PRIZE-WINNING oil paintings

AND <u>WHY</u> THEY WON THE PRIZE

by
margaret harold

with comments
by
gus baker

designed
by
harold g. oliphant

The painting shown on jacket is the
Prize-Winning painting, Linear Structure,
by Herbert Bayer

CONSULTANTS: Reginald Poland, Gus Baker,
George Dutch and John Sellers

ALLIED PUBLICATIONS, INC., PUBLISHERS

Library of Congress Catalog Card No. 60-53333

Jacket printed on 100-lb. offset enamel. Body printed on 100-lb. Warren's dull-coated enamel, with 9 pt. Electra type. Color separations by Sun Litho Plate Co., Cincinnati, Ohio.

Lithographed by The Parthenon Press, Nashville, Tennessee, U.S.A.

preface

So far as we know, this is the first time the general public has been offered an opportunity to view the top prize-winning paintings from the major competitions throughout the nation. Before this, the only index of current painting activity, the experimentation as well as the conservatism, has had to come by way of travelling exhibits, the galleries and museums in New York, the art periodicals, and the art columns in various other publications. Obviously, this was not complete; and just as obviously, it was not the fault of the exhibitions, galleries, museums, or publications . . . for with the increase in the number of people's painting in the country, and the great number of prizes, purchase awards, and honorable mentions in each competition, all of these multiplied by the number of *fields* of art, such an ambitious survey would require a staff as ponderous as that of an encyclopedia. Nor do we think such a ponderous survey even desirable, for undoubtedly it would leave us just as confused as to directions of painting as do some of the national competitions.

Our scope, then, is limited to the field of *oil paintings*—and we present in this volume the winner of the first prize (or top purchase award) in each of forty-eight important exhibitions.

In studying this book, the reader should be aware of the fact that in no case did the writer of the Comments see or otherwise know the contents of the Statement by the Artist. For that reason there may be disagreement between Artist and Commentator. In other cases there is remarkable agreement between them. But neither saw the other's writing until after actual publication of this book.

It is our hope that the statement by the artist will clarify some of the obscurity concerning the before and after process of the act of painting the picture. Thus the reader will be able to form his own opinion of how well the intention of the painter is realized in the painting, whether it falls short—or, as in the case of most fine paintings, exceeded the conscious intent of the artist.

In the process of teaching, painting, and looking at paintings we, between us, have arrived at the conclusion that there is no real means, no verbal language in which you can say why you *like* a painting. Liking a picture involves so much of the emotional complexes that whatever words come out tend to demonstrate how much of what we feel is irrational by any accepted standard of logic.

The following are some of the means we have employed in assessing the value and excellence of a painting.

First, we have tried to see the painting in the context of the tradition out of which it springs. No painting can come into being that does not owe something to the past. This past is either built upon or revolted against; in either case, there is a debt. These debts may be in the form of academic training, the use of painting materials, theory of color, design and space.

Second, there is a rational basis for every painting, even though the content may spring from the irrational. The irrational may be thought of in this case to be similar to a literary conceit or a metaphor, the validity of which imagewise is not justified until the work is produced. The rational content expresses itself in the design and composition of the picture. Composition in this sense is neither good nor bad, nor is it intellectually imposed on the subject matter. Rather, it is the abstract, pictorial means whereby the event of the painting is recreated, whether it be psychical, non-figurative painting or one executed with direct reference to the natural world.

Third, a painting contains a distillation of experience. This experience may come from other paintings, from nature, or from the other arts. It may begin with nature and go to abstraction or generalities, or the process may be reversed according to intention of the painter. It may proceed, like Gris, from abstraction to object.

Fourth, every painting begins with an intention even though there are schools (such as the school of automatism) which deny it. In a situation of this nature, the enjoyment of materials becomes the intention. But an intention, being of the nature of an idea, is not a painting. Consequently, there is a hypothetical relationship involved wherein the artist sets up a guess and proceeds to find out whether the result works or not.

Fifth, good painting does not have symbols, but adds up to a symbol. It is from this symbol that the parts must be judged. We have heard this principle described in many ways. One that has intrigued us with its simplicity is that at one point a painting ceases to be competent—and something magical happens. Another way, a painter can put two and two together and get five, but it takes an artist to get six. All of these seem to say that the totality is more than the sum of its parts, that the artist has produced the unexpected —and, as Conrad put it, we receive some of the "truth for which we forgot to ask."

However pedantic these principles may sound, they are the means by which we have looked at the paintings. We have tried to be completely honest in our statements and to address ourselves to what was in the painting first, scrupulously avoiding the reading into it of personal meanings. By no stretch of the imagination can a work of art be explained.

•

The forty-eight paintings shown in this book were the winners of the 1959 competitions. Those which won in the 1960 competitions will be shown in next year's volume, to be designated Book II. Thus the 1959 paintings shown in this present volume constitute the first of a series of annuals. Book II is in preparation as this present Book I goes to press.

In addition, the publishers have in preparation the first volume of a series of annuals on prize-winning water colors . . . and the first of a series of annuals on prize-winning graphics.

•

The editors and publishers welcome the comments, criticisms, suggestions, and assistance of all artists, museum and gallery officials, teachers of art, art critics, and the editors of those splendid art magazines with which we are blessed. We invite their participation with us in the pleasure of bringing the topmost prize winners up for examination and discussion by all who are interested in the world of art.

reginald poland

W e must know modern art . . . any art . . . to appreciate it. The best way to know art is to associate with it at firsthand. Museums, in offering annually a juried, competitive show of an appreciable area, and with generous awards, give anyone interested a chance to see many different creations in different styles and a chance to make comparisons.

Since art should visually express artists' reaction to life, in ways to interest, enrich, stimulate and perhaps please the beholder, these large, regional and seasonal shows hold a real value.

One person may prefer a Norman Rockwell interpretation of "homely homey" American life, another a Steig, humorous glimpse of our "small-fry" cooking-up trouble for an unsuspecting "Pollyanna." A third type of gallery visitor might delight in a surrealistic Salvador Dali of "wilted watches" that are symbolic in the matter of time. Many people are drawn to the abstract variations played on any of these themes. Each gets something valuable, a step forward, to either side, or even backward. But all are life-enhancing, which is the goal of all art.

No one is expected to react favorably to all he will find; art is an individual matter. Any art work which makes a contribution to some often proves distasteful to others. Therein lies something of art's unique significance. And since each art annual is quite varied, its offerings ordinarily provide something of value to each beholder who retains an open mind.

Reginald Poland
Director of Museums
Atlanta, Georgia

josef albers

SEEING   ART

Art is not   to be looked at

art is looking   at us

What is art   to others

is not necessarily art to me

nor   for the same reason

and vice versa

What was   art to me

or was not   some time ago

might have lost   that value

or gained it   in the meantime

and maybe   again

Thus art is not   an object

but   experience

To be able   to perceive it

we need to be   receptive

Therefore art is   there

where art   seizes us

by

Josef Albers

contents

AWARD-WINNING ARTISTS

AWARD-WINNING ARTISTS—Continued

Continued next page

AWARD-WINNING ARTISTS—Continued

contents

EXHIBITIONS

Continued next page

EXHIBITIONS—Continued

EXHIBITIONS—Continued

garo z.
antreasian

Mr. Antreasian is presently "Master Printer" at Tamarind Lithographic Workshop for Professional and Research Development, in Los Angeles, California. He is listed in Who's Who in American Art.

statement by the artist

During the period when *Tropicana* was conceived and executed, I was interested in producing a series of paintings about non-specific places that had a rather specific aura of geographical locale. Thus *Tropicana*, while not depicting an exact place, embodies the flavor of many similar places. The emphasis is placed on the feeling or sentiment in the picture, which in itself might be called its true "subject matter".

The attempt was to produce this particular semi-tropical aura in a big and splendorous way. A highly suggestive coloring was used, as well as full and lazy forms. The painting style is an ebullient one that suggests the spirit and pure joy of painting in itself. Perhaps the essence of this joy is the same as that of the kind of place it depicts. Bringing such spirited "life" to the work is for one the most difficult problems of all and my ever-present challenge.

critic's comments

Heat, light, and opulence, these are the feelings and sensations caught in this painting. The still life, which on first examination seems to be the subject of the picture, later becomes the vehicle for introducing the conceptions to the audience, much as a prologue does in a play or a poem. The plastic, thematic materials are all here, the color and color harmonies, the line, the shapes, the textures as well as the painter's handwriting.

The main problem in the picture is the relation of the still life to a background which from object size is in deep space. Conventional perspective is disregarded, for obviously this is a condition where the recession must not be stated lest the painter lose control. It must be implied only, hence maintaining the integrity of the plane. The diagonals of the table are the only lines used to suggest depth. Other means are used instead of lines, the clockwise movement of the plates, beginning near the center of the painting, moving left and ending with the glasses on the right; the diminishing size of the objects and the reduction of contrasts. The picture plane is maintained by a series of vertical brush strokes, moving in a larger clockwise motion with the plates. The importance of the strokes can scarcely be overemphasized, for they continue to bring the eye back to the surface of the picture, while in the background they serve as reflections in the water.

tropicana by Garo Z. Antreasian. Top award in Indiana Artists Exhibition, The John Herron Art Museum, Indianapolis, Indiana.

statement by critic

The judges, in this case, undoubtedly found the artist's style quite satisfying. Notice the unity of his composition . . . the balance, the serenity.

judges

Fred Conway, Washington University, St. Louis, Missouri; Herbert P. Barnett, Dean, Art Academy of Cincinnati, Ohio.

herbert bayer

Mr. Bayer is now Consultant Designer for Container Corporation of America. He lives in Aspen, Colorado. He is listed in Who's Who in American Art.

statement by the artist

My paintings are usually inspired by nature experience, but this is not necessarily so in the case of *Linear Structure*. As I make no distinction of value or quality between organic and geometric forms, I sometimes express this experience visually with geometric-abstract elements. The line is one of these elements which have fascinated me for years. Linear motives have occupied many of my compositions, and I have returned to them after having painted works of a quite different nature.

The subject of the painting, although not supported by the title, is obviously space, and as the canvas is limited to a two-dimensional plane, it must be space as an illusion. The two black oblongs are sometimes seen as free-floating planes, sometimes as windows. The space is not immutably fixed by perspectives with a vanishing point in the distance but is created by feelings of a vacuum around and between the design elements. The receding effect of blue supports this illusion. The partial transparency of the lines and their meeting with the black oblongs make a distinction between the traditional foreground and background doubtful.

There is a structural order expressed in the composition. The casual grouping of lines is evolving into a system of horizontals and verticals without becoming static.

This is an intellectual explanation of my painting. There is, however, beyond this rational analysis, a metaphysical quality which I am not attempting to describe, as I would rather have it convey itself upon the viewer.

critic's comments

Twentieth century "Neo-Realists" make a distinction concerning ideas or geometrical shapes that is very important when we are confronted by a painting employing these shapes. The theory originates with Plato, that there are these archetypal ideas which are pure subsist but do not exist in the realm of pure being. This word, "subsist", means that the idea is neither patient nor agent, nor has any position in space or time. Once the idea of a triangle becomes an existing triangle it not only becomes specific but is subject to generation and decay in space and in time. Therefore, no sensory triangle can be the pure idea. I do not think this painting makes that mistake of attempting to violate such a distinction.

One might think that in dealing with such objective subject matter as geometrical configurations personal style would automatically suffer, and emotion be completely eliminated. Those who have had the experience of teaching know that neither is the case.

In most design classes this much symmetry in a painting would be abhorred. But here it is used with good reason, for the painting is really a theme with variations, with the balance used as a second statement of the theme to clarify the variations. The painter has used the geometrical in much the same way as Francis Bacon's variations on Velazquez's "Pope Innocent X", but with this major difference: Bacon relies on our memory of the Velazquez to effect his variations; Bayer does not; the restatement of the theme is within the picture.

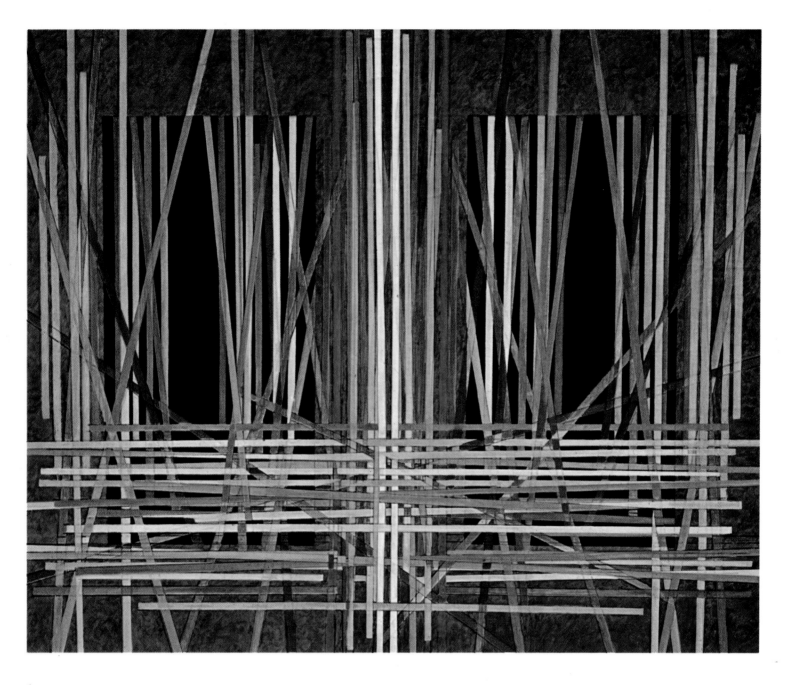

linear structure by Herbert Bayer. Top award in Southwest American Painting Exhibition, Oklahoma Art Center, Oklahoma City, Oklahoma.

statement by critic

This is indisputably a prize piece of art. Observe the harmony of colors, the simplicity of design . . . and note, too, the complete avoidance of all formulas . . . and you'll see why this painting captivated the judge.

judge

Gordon Bailey Washburn, Director of Fine Arts, Carnegie Institute.

george beattie

Mr. Beattie is now a lecturer and professor of free-hand drawing at the School of Architecture, Georgia Tech., and is also associated with the Atlanta Art Institute, Atlanta, Georgia.

statement by the artist

My philosophy of painting is firmly centered in the Christian belief that God is the creator and ruler of the Universe, and from Him stems all truth, beauty and creative freedom. I believe in the dignity of honest creative ingenuity as justified by the Christian conscience.

As to this particular painting, I wanted to express here the unity of the three buildings of the Pisa group . . . the Leaning Tower, the Baptistry, and the Cathedral . . . and to express this unity as an architectural jewel carved in some precious stone. I used the nocturnal mood to enhance the luminous antiquity of this gem as set apart from the surrounding world.

critic's comments

The fact that some architecture has been called "frozen music" makes the title of this painting, *Italian Nocturne*, particularly appropriate. Mozart, Field, and Chopin all used the title for their meditative compositions. However, Chopin frequently interrupted the dream-like melodic line for a strong dramatic contrast and development.

The fact that the painting is devoid of strong color and depends on the value of contrasts for its impact focuses the feeling of night. If we ask ourselves, could this not be a stormy day with the light breaking through the clouds and illuminating just this isolated group of buildings, we would be forced to admit that such is highly improbable, for the cool colors would have a greater color variation and the buildings even more dramatically shaded in light and dark. Further, the painter tells us in the abstract elements of the painting that this is not to be taken literally, for on examination the buildings become transparent; lines are projected into the sky and the landscape around the buildings to emphasize this point.

Plastically, the problem of the upper left corner is solved by the circle of the moon, and could be considered the full statement of the theme which undergoes all the variations throughout the arches in the buildings, with the straight-line projections functioning as a contrasting accompaniment.

The major thrust of the painting is from the foreground base of the buildings toward the upper right corner of the painting. This thrust tends to pull the moon down on a diagonal from the upper left corner toward the buildings. It is arrested in its movement by the projected line of the tower.

The total mystic effect of the painting is enhanced by the feeling that the buildings are floating in a sea of night air, and are ever so tenuously anchored in space.

italian nocturne by George Beattie. Top award in Mead-Atlanta *Painting of the Year Exhibition*, Atlanta, Georgia.

statement by judge

Mr. George Beattie's painting *Italian Nocturne* seemed to me to have all the requirements of a prize-winning picture . . . fine draughtsmanship, good use of color plus that mysterious relationship between the art of the past and the present that makes a work of art of lasting importance.

VINCENT PRICE, Judge

judges

Vincent Price, Los Angeles; Agnes Morgan, Cambridge, Massachusetts; Joseph de Martini, New York City; Reginald Poland, Director, High Museum of Art, Atlanta, Georgia.

rosemary browne beck

Mrs. Beck is now living in Indianapolis, Indiana with her husband, Richard Beck, and their two sons. Mr. Beck is an Art Director for Eli Lilly Co.

statement by the artist

Art, for me, must not be overly organized or contrived. I do not admire those who paint certain things in certain ways which they know to be popular, or who place undue importance on any of the techniques of painting for their own sakes: such as, novel or exaggerated application of paint, or mathematically contrived design. These are academic considerations which should be instinctive for the artist by the time he has become mature.

For example, though this is oversimplifying, one should not have to say to oneself, "I will paint an abstraction of a tree. It will be effective on a long narrow canvas, perhaps placed in a startling arrangement." It would be far better to say, "This tree inspires me. I must paint what I feel about it. I must show its strength, its dignity." And then, one, while painting the tree, might begin to simplify the form, to erase detail for emphasis and purity, making abstraction his natural means of expression.

While one painter abstracts his subject matter to clarify it, the other dwells on and enhances the intricacies and nuances to make the painting meaningful. Both painters, though their methods of expression are different, have the same purpose: that of enriching the viewer . . . increasing his sensitivity to any and all the phases of life.

As all this regards my *Still Life*, I believe it is pretty apparent that I am a painter of the latter breed . . . one who loves to tickle out to the extreme all that will make my objects more intriguing. Light falling intricately on drapery fascinates me. Each tiny shadow is mysterious and beguiling. This painting was the first upon which I'd used artificial light, and I found that my work did not seem to suffer from it, as I had feared it might. Now I enjoy painting at night; there is a stillness in the air and an unhurried quality in my being; my power of concentration can be focused entirely upon my subject and the feelings it evokes in me.

critic's comments

The opulent still life became popular during the period of the Dutch "little masters," wherein the technical proficiency and polish was so high as to include a vast array of differentiated textures such as gold, glass, veined foliage and blossoms, fruits as well as insects and drops of water. It is surprising that with such a plenitude any degree of quietness in the composition could be achieved. Opposed to this opulence are the still lifes of Chardin, which are more classical in feeling.

The present "Still Life" we are viewing has something of both, being classical in its color restraint. But the many rhythms of the lines and planes in the cloth as well as the objects add up to an opulent feeling.

The problem that the artist has posed does not end with the question of how to paint white eggs in a white bowl on a white cloth, but to include a white goblet and a white plate as well. The highest color saturation is in the yellow of the lemons, with the color being repeated in a lower key in the background drapery. Gray violet shadow tones are used throughout to emphasize the yellow tonality and character of the light, which is being slightly influenced by the background and the two modified triangles of the foreground. The space is skillfully created and controlled by the angular convergences of the folds of the cloth and the modulated contrasts of value and color.

still life by Rosemary Browne Beck. Top award in Hoosier Salon, Auditorium Galleries of the William H. Block Co., Indianapolis.

statements by the judges

The jury selected this painting for many reasons: (1) Excellent design pattern that was well organized; (2) Good color, plus much attention to texture and solidity; (3) Most important . . . very good draughtsmanship . . . skillfully handled . . . . I consider her work (this canvas) very, very good.

STEPHEN G. MANIATTY, Judge
Chuck Willow Studio
Old Deerfield, Mass.

. . . I found the still life painting . . . the best composed and organized . . . . It was the best in that class in color, form, control, good craftsmanship and neat presentation as a total picture.

PETER PAUL DUBANIEWICZ, Judge
Cleveland Institute of Art
Cleveland, Ohio

. . . it stood out from the many other good things in the show. The color and design were very good, as was the composition.

WALTER PARKE, Judge
Libertyville, Illinois

john j. bednar

Mr. Bednar is currently teaching drawing, painting and sculpture at the South Bend Art Association and Indiana University Extension of South Bend-Mishawaka, Indiana.

statement by the artist

I believe that the public (and probably many artists) should be made aware that painting and drawing are two separate fields of the art world, not one. Correct drawing, like grammar, can be learned by anyone because basically drawing is concerned with the construction of things in proper perspective. Painting is concerned first with design, so that drawing becomes subordinate to design. The drawing is conditioned or altered as the design requires. Color is the vehicle by which this design is usually executed. But the proper distribution of color is also regulated by the design. We have immortal Chinese paintings with little or no use of color, and we also have a thousand-year-long period of pre-da Vinci art which disregarded correctness of drawing, of anatomy, perspective and light and shade. The great periods of Medieval Byzantine, Egyptian, and Persian art were based on design, not on drawing. This stress on design does not imply that one cannot produce great painting when correct drawing is employed, but that correct drawing must be held constantly in its proper relationship, or better, subordination, to design.

The *Portrait of Mr. Radecki* gave me particular pleasure of execution because here I had a rugged, dynamic individual, a painter and craftsman, familiar with the problems of the artist. He gave me complete freedom to paint him as I saw him, with no punches pulled to record the surface appearance and the intangible personality underneath. This kind of freedom is rare, for in most cases the commissioned portrait must please the sitter, not the artist, and the result too often is a good likeness but a poor work of art. Many artists avoid the field of portraiture so as not to compromise themselves. I was fortunate in having an understanding model.

critic's comments

The handling of this portrait dates back to Brouwer and Hals, of the Flemish and Dutch school respectively. For it was primarily during the Western Renaissance that this particular type of portrait came into vogue, reflecting the activities and tastes of the rising middle class. Subject matter no longer had to be the nobility, Biblical, or based on Classical mythology to be suitable for painting, and with astonishing virtuosity and ease the Flemish and Dutch painters recorded their times as they saw and experienced them.

There are two debts to Hals in this portrait. First, the seeming informality, as though the painter had an instantaneous technique comparable to the camera in its ability to capture the fleeting and critical moment of intensity. Second, the handling of the brush, wherein the distinction that this is a painting is not lost; rather the portrait, on close examination, breaks into discreet brush marks, and the image is not recreated until the spectator backs away from the painting. It was Rembrandt who insisted that his portraits were to be looked at, not smelled.

It is certainly a fact that most portraits lose a great deal of their vitality once the artist attempts to smooth and fuse the brush strokes. Leaving the brush strokes showing in both the figure and the background aids immeasurably in making this portrait a unity.

portrait of mr. radecki by John J. Bednar. Top award in Michigan Art Exhibition, South
Bend Art Center, South Bend, Indiana.

statement by critic

Here is an artist who knows how to remain scrupulously exact
without being banal. Notice, too, the purity and sharpness of insight
and you'll see why the judge put his coveted stamp on this one.

the judge

William D. Peat, Director John Herron Art Museum.

wayne begley

Mr. Begley has recently participated in the exhibition of "Ten American Artists in Rome" at the Palazzo Venezia, Rome, Italy.

statement by the artist

A work of art must always be dynamic, activistic, and full of frenzy. Not in the politician's sense of an inciting to action nor in the popular sense of unbridled irresponsibility, but rather, its frenzy must be like the mystic's furied, visionary self-excitement to perfect and significant inaction. This state, produced by the work of art, causes every consideration of the viewer to vibrate electrically and harmoniously in accord.

A painting, then, can never be just an open window on the real world or the soul. Its impact must be forthcoming . . . a projection of its exuberant qualities upon the fabric of the viewer. Yet paradoxically the painting must also include the viewer within itself. It must create a space, a stage for the dramatic and aesthetic happening. A space also that grants to the viewer's perception a foothold from which he may be aware of the painting's identity as both separate and one with him.

Again, the dynamism of the painting does not exclude the necessity of unity . . . of co-ordinated and coherent dynamic forms . . . from that painting's effect. Unity in the face of frenzy is achieved by a constant retreat and compromise which strengthens and expands the dramatic scope of the painting rather than diminishing it. *Tandava*, or the cosmic dance of Shiva, expresses in Hindu thought the seemingly reckless dynamism of the universe. Reeling between flagrant destruction and the phoenix-like consequences of his acts, the artist must cope with these dualistic urges of life and strive to achieve, and through his frenzy to make way for a never-ending ordering and recreation of experience.

critic's comments

In thinking of the influence the Orient has had on Western painting, probably the first that comes into our mind is the change wrought by Japanese prints on the painting of Whistler and Van Gogh and Gauguin. Now we may think of the picture writing of Mark Tobey and Franz Kline, writing which goes beyond word designation and seeks to form a cognate for a whole emotional complex. Few who have seen Mark Tobey's *Edge of August* will doubt its evocative powers.

In *Tandava* another influence is taking place, reversing the influence felt in India at Gandhara by Greek culture under the aegis of Alexander, and later by the Roman Empire. *Tandava* represents the Indian influence on the West. But it differs from the previous Oriental influences in that the calligraphy maintains its Indian meaning even though it is the basis of the plastic composition.

The concept of line which the Greeks carried to India was not the line of the archaic Apollos but the line tending toward naturalism that we see in late vase painting and in the Pompeian frescoes. It was a deliberate attempt to conquer the contingencies of time and position. Although the Indian sculptures employed the technique, the art never went to the lengths of naturalism that we find in late Hellenistic and Roman works. The restraining factor in India was the

tandava by Wayne Begley. Top award in Louisville Art Center Exhibition, J. B. Speed Art Museum, Louisville, Kentucky.

already-abstracted meaning existing in music and the dance and the figure as such was subjected to these disciplines.

To some observers *Tandava* may appear to be a gopura, or temple gate, highly ornamented with abstract dancing figures with its two uprights leaving the composition at the bottom. But a richer interpretation follows the assumption that the composition is based on the symbolic syllable AUM ओं which is a visual equivalent of Tandava, the cosmic dance of Shiva, which includes four states of consciousness: A—consciousness when awake; U—dream consciousness; M—dreamless sleep. And finally the silence around the sacred syllable is the Unmanifest Transcedent.

Should one wish to go further, the center portion of the painting could be interpreted as waking consciousness, for the configurations are much more definite in this area. The areas with bluer tints could be the dream-conscious state. The darker portions could signify dreamless sleep. Outside, the syllable in the composition could certainly imply the silence, thus completing the interpretation.

statement by the judge

. . . a very authoritative painter. So many people are painting large paintings, but this is big enough for the canvas.

PHILIP R. ADAMS, Director
Cincinnati Art Museum

claude
bentley

Mr. Bentley is now Instructor at the Art Institute
of Chicago, members group, lecture series;
Instructor, creative painting, Old Town Art
Center; and Instructor, creative painting,
Contemporary Art Workshop, Chicago, Illinois.
He is listed in Who's Who in American Art.

statement by the artist

My paintings have no pre-determined plan. They are resolved on
the canvas. Their source may be subconscious, intuitive, unknown.
I wish to complete a painting in the shortest period of time in
order to preserve the initial impulse. The result may invoke an
image or be an adventure for the eye. Titles are for purposes of
identification, are afterthoughts, and should not create a limitation
for the spectator.

critic's comments

One of the effects of the "newly discovered" African art by the
Fauves, and later by Picasso, has been the deeper appreciation of art
forms from the more remote regions of the world. In common par-
lance, the word "primitive" is used to describe these various forms,
and yet from the aspect of skill and conception, they are far from
being crude.

Various syntheses have been attempted . . . Gauguin with Bre-
tonnese and Oceanic art, Picasso with Iberian sculpture and African
masks, Chagall with Russian folk-art and folklore, Tamayao with his
own Mayan heritage.

There is something of the shock of a New Hebrides Fetish in this
painting, *Plumed Serpent*, with the eyeless sockets of the serpent head
emerging from its brightly colored decoration. This emergence is
caused by the strong contrast in light and dark at the bottom of the
picture, with the angular direction of the lines of the head converging
into the background. It is this tension of the converging lines which
prevents the head from violating the plane of the picture. The color
areas serve not only as an arresting contrast, but serve as the transi-
tional area between the head and the calligraphic architecture of the
background.

In examining the history of painting from the Renaissance to the
turn of the century, one could arrive at a theory of the aesthetics
of the period by the dominance of an idea so general that it is not
overlooked so much as it is taken for granted. The idea is this: that
each painting contains a point of reference to the objective, natural
world. Leonardo saw this in his attempts to create monsters, for the
monster becomes a composite of shapes derived from other animals.
Whether it is the fantastic world of Bosch, or the classical world of
David, the imagery was still derived from the visual world, and served
as a point of reference, to reinforce a system of relationships which
could serve equally well as fiction or fact.

With this point of reference came the problem of how to represent
form in space; and though the problem was chiefly solved by Leonardo,
painters continued to build on the deductions from Leonardo's
theories. To a great extent, the space which this aesthetic entailed was
not challenged until Cezanne, whose concept of space we find reducing the autonomy of the image and thereby switching the degree of
importance of the point of reference or the old aesthetic to the new
importance of picture as painting. This prepared the field for the
discovery of "primitive painting".

plumed serpent by Claude Bentley. Top award in National Exhibition, John and Mable Ringling Art Museum, Sarasota, Florida.

statement by judge

I gave the top prize in the 1959 Annual National Exhibition at Sarasota, Florida to Claude Bentley's painting for the following reasons: It is a handsome and an arresting painting executed with much authority. It has beautiful and subtle color and is seen abstractly, in the contemporary style with complete understanding and well-balanced composition. What is more, it has a spirited quality that seems vividly reminiscent of the *Plumed Serpent*.

ADELYN D. BREESKIN, Director,
Baltimore Museum of Art

judges

Adelyn D. Breeskin, Awards Juror, Director, Baltimore Museum of Art, Baltimore, Maryland; Katherine Kuhl, Art Institute of Chicago, Chicago, Illinois; Jerry Bywaters, Dallas Museum of Fine Arts, Dallas, Texas; Richard Brown, Los Angeles County Museum, Los Angeles, California; John I. L. Baur, Whitney Museum of American Art, New York City, New York; Dr. Creighton Gilbert, John and Mable Ringling Museum of Art, Sarasota, Florida.

mary bryan

Mrs. Bryan and her husband, Alden Bryan, have studios and a summer art gallery in Gloucester, Massachusetts, and spend winters in Jeffersonville, Vermont. They are both listed in Who's Who in American Art.

statement by the artist

The original idea for the painting *Stowe Village* came from a watercolor sketch that I had made sometime before. The watercolor was executed in an open manner, using broad color washes surrounded by intervals of white paper.

The basic idea in the sketch had been to express the vast proportions of the towering mountain compared to the tiny village below.

Actually, the subject was ideally suited to a large canvas, affording the opportunity of further exploring the bold masses and planes of the mountain. Furthermore, the accentuation of the rugged masses was suggested by the white paper.

I decided to retain the vignette appearance of the sketch to increase the enclosed feeling around the village. The foreground areas were treated in large simple forms to heighten this effect. The color and values of sky and snow were closely related for the same reason, though they had to be given sufficient form and interest to create a unity of design throughout the picture plane. They were also a vital element in causing a sensation of space surrounding the mountain and village.

Nearly all my paintings in any medium are done without drawing or lay-in on the working surface. Lines tend to distract me and disturb the mental image. I start to paint directly with the palette knife, working from the center of interest and establishing the basic forms of the composition as rapidly as possible. These forms are painted as areas, not indicated in drawing, and are related to each other in size, volume, and tension.

Whenever a picture reaches a point where I no longer feel keyed up, I usually lay it aside for a time. This procedure usually results in a reevaluation of the problems that were formerly troubling me and a renewed interest in the subject.

critic's comments

Aristotle's unities of time, place, and action functioned to translate a dramatic micro-cosmos into a macro-cosmos. Over and over in the literature and painting of the day, we find the same dramatic device used for an intensification that gathers from the forces combined of reduction of accidentals and astute focus on the thematic materials. By this process of simplification and elimination, the part implies the whole. There is a curiosity and fear connected with self-knowledge, a feeling that if the sphere of activity were suddenly narrowed, and that sphere small enough to be known, the individual could at last see himself . . . hence, the fascination of *Robinson Crusoe*, *The Magic Mountain*, Rembrandt's *Man in the Gold Helmet*, Vermeer's *The Artist in His Studio*.

This painting deals with a natural isolation, a village in the mountains locked in by snow. The composition is an "s" curve, which is flattened in from and extended by the mountains to prevent excessive recession in depth. The area of the village is the only polychromatic passage of color, for the remaining areas of the picture take their tonal cast, either from the mountain or from the warm areas of the village.

stowe village by Mary Bryan. Top award in Allied Artists of America, National Academy Galleries, New York City.

statement by critic

The painter's keenness for ideas undoubtedly led to the award in this instance. She treats her subject matter with more complex significance than simple landscapes or still life.

jury of awards

Walter Farndon, Chairman, Douglaston, New York; Greta Matson, Brooklyn, New York; Henry Bankoff, New York City.

31

tom cavanaugh

Mr. Cavanaugh is now a member of the faculty at Louisiana State University, Department of Fine Arts, Baton Rouge, Louisiana. He is also the Director and owner of the Bay Street Studio, Boothbay Harbor, Maine.

statement by the artist

During the passive and active stages of executing a painting, I maintain an attitude of respect for the objective nature of the theme, and I search for the possible interest which its inherent character may reveal. At the same time, my subjective responses must be evaluated, not arbitrarily, but on terms suggested by the theme. An ordered introspection, thus projected and then qualified, acts as a stabilizer in my creative process. I try to avoid direct decisions and statements stemming from my known abilities and studio experience.

I recently have noticed that a single idea pervades all of my painting: the dynamic effect of environment upon experience. Environment, whether interpreted as forces of weather, noise, social pressure, occupation or evolution, is dominant in every situation.

I never have felt a strong compulsion to paint my immediate environment just because I happened to be on the scene. Only after some time has passed, subsequent to my experience within a situation, am I able to transform its thematic material into a personal response for painting. This process of assimilation often results in peculiar easel habits: that of painting Maine in Italy, or of painting Italy in Louisiana.

The painting, Beach Walk, contains elements from my most painted themes, the figure and the sea. The asymetrical composition resulted from the intended content rather than by plan. The painting was intended to convey certain qualities and overtones: an exhilarating experience, vicariously recalled; brisk wind and opalescent beach light; self-imposed solitude; poetic and heroic effects of Nature upon Man; Man's affinity and coexistence with the sea.

critic's comments

Verisimilitude, or the attempt to render natural appearances, is a term that is often used interchangeably with "realism". Both terms frequently end in confusion: Verisimilitude, even with the intent to be completely objective and faithful to every detail in nature, will automatically include some stylization which will be over and above the negative aspect of simple eliminations (which may or may not be the result of conscious intent).

The realist, though he realizes the importance of appearances, is more of a searcher after structure, that which binds appearances together. That structure may be formal or conceptual, bound up with the nature of picture-making. Or it may be the structure of experience which he is trying to clarify, or finally the structure of things in nature. Naturally none of these aspects is mutually exclusive.

The design in Beach Walk is a re-creation of an experience. The movements involved are directly related to the figure, whose directional movement is from left to right. This movement is further implemented by the triangles pointing inward on the right-hand side, as well as the diagonal from upper left stretching to lower right. Rather than concentrating on appearance, the artist has used poetic analogies: the sky is like a ragged curtain, the driftwood like grasping fingers, the sand is soft like the cloud; and, finally, humanity is like driftwood, having no roots, subject to the forces that are larger, though unconscious, than he is.

beach walk by Tom Cavanaugh. Top award in Exhibition of the Art Association of New Orleans, Isaac Delgado Museum of Art, New Orleans, Louisiana.

statement by juror

The painting *Beach Walk* interested me, even from the time of my first seeing it among the hundreds of others submitted to the jury. Although it was by no means as bright in color or as large in size as many of the other paintings, it invited my interest and promised a rich, visual experience. This promise was subsequently fulfilled in a way commensurate with the quality of the invitation first extended. This alone is something to value in a work of art.

The means employed by Mr. Cavanaugh appeared eminently well suited to the subject and to what I felt the artist intended as import. From all visual evidence it was clear to me that the artist is a competent craftsman able to keep his craft in the service of artistic expression of a high order.

Beach Walk appeared to me as one of those happy performances in which form and subject work to a single end . . . the expression of a content alive with the feeling of human existence in nature.

DONALD L. WEISMANN, Professor of Art
The University of Texas, Austin 12, Texas

jurors

Donald L. Weismann, Professor of Art, The University of Texas, Austin 12, Texas; Creighton Gilbert, Director, Ringling Museum, Sarasota, Florida.

33

leonard edmondson

Mr. Edmondson is now Instructor in Art at Pasadena City College, Pasadena, California. He is listed in Who's Who in American Art.

statement by the artist

My recent painting has a technique directed toward a revelation of movement through gesture, color opposition (vibration), and ambiguity of spatial position. These visual devices are developed to produce an optical space. My painting grows out of a need to express intuitive, emphathetic needs basic to the fundamental humanness implicit in all mankind. Since my work is always abstract and often non-figurative, the means to formulate an effective image begins with automatic drawing and remains completely non-intellectually determined until, in the final states, certain adjustments of color are made.

I feel that my value as a painter lies in revealing a personal world which in turn becomes, when it is complete, a universal world.

critic's comments

How much is lost in the realm of living today when we accept as the only truth the literal, the factual, the scientific description of events? There was a time when conversation was a fine art, and the mutual exchange of ideas could occur in embroidered stories, parables and allegories. The fictions involved were simply the vehicle for clothing the insight into matters deeper than outward correspondence provided.

The color in this painting could be found in the Egyptian temples, in the Etruscan tombs, or in a Minoan palace. And, in truth, the color is employed on the surface of the picture very much as though it were just such a mural painting. This point of recall adds and reinforces the conception of "a legend," that this is from the past. On impulse one might say that the shapes are from Klee, but we would prefer to consider that this painting drew from the same source as Klee, that is, children's art. But the control, complexity and design are certainly not childlike. They are highly skilled.

Just as in Egyptian painting, the planes are all parallel to the picture surface, there are pictographic symbols of earth, fields, trees and bushes. It is the movement and insistence on the linear treatment which gives the feeling of a journey. The color in the lower and right-hand side of the painting is happy and without anxiety or apprehension.

The color is friendly, although the shapes and movement give a feeling of a topsy-turvy world. But this is necessary, for without it, the looming dark shapes whose character suggests fear would disturb the ultimate equilibrium of the painting.

a legend by Leonard Edmondson. *Top award in the San Gabriel Valley Artists Exhibition, Pasadena Art Museum, Pasadena, California.*

statements by the jurors

As to Edmondson's *A Legend* . . . let me say that it is another painting in a career devoted to a search for those elements which relate himself to nature. His chosen method appears to be in the use of colorful, essentially flat amorphous forms designed and placed in a manner remote and compelling. Familiarity with this unique and wonderful idiom invites endless contemplation. The spectator is transported to a strange and romantic world only to realize he is experiencing a brilliant intensification of his own existence.

JOHN McLAUGHLIN
Dana Point, California

The particular qualities which attracted me to Mr. Edmondson's painting are the confident organization of the deliberate forms bending and extending over the surface to suggest movement in a fluid world . . . the space of this composition. With irregular and almost awkward edges, the forms compactly yet freely overlap near the center and open up toward the edges in an organic life of attraction and withdrawal. With amazing subtlety and variety, the character of the forms and their speed· of movement are contrasted at times as in the very elongated areas and sharp points of black; and reinforced at other times as in the angular, bright red and bulky green areas. I also like the way the artist, using the frame to isolate a small, anonymous drama, composed the picture to suggest that the groping and exploratory action is continuous with that of a larger world.

JAMES ELLIOTT
Los Angeles County Museum

35

william lee
freeland

Mr. Freeland is now
living in West Chester,
Pennsylvania.

statement by the artist

So much has been said already today about painting and painters,
but it all leads to one truth . . . painting is a visual experience. I feel
that many think that, possibly, in all of the millions of words about
art that are to be found in newspapers, books and abridged weekly
magazines, the key or secret route will be found to the understanding
of what is being done today with this new painting. Time spent reading all of this entertaining material brings one no closer to the truth,
for one must view the work itself, for it tells, or strives to tell, what the
painter is about.

Painting is a working process . . . not a preconceived thinking and
working process. I have not decided anything upon beginning a
painting, for the painting is to tell me what I am about; I cannot
tell the painting. Painting must be a first-hand experience, not a diluted one.

I have been asked what led to my painting *Margurite's*. I can
only answer this by saying that my being a painter led to this expression. At the completion of this canvas I experienced an emotional
response from it similar to one received at the home of one named
Margurite. When I smell old musty books, I recall a certain ten-year
period of my life . . . an aged and ill grandfather, a chained wooden
porch swing, a dirt-floor cellar, a white frame Huntington, West
Virginia home. I recall this visually and emotionally. Emotionally, it
is something alive and fresh; visually, diluted. This painting had the
emotional smell of Margurite's.

critic's comments

Unlike many of the movements in modern painting, "expressionism" had no program, no specifically planned aesthetic, nor was
it conducive to binding artists together into a group movement.
Rather, the one constant of the movement was its individualism,
springing from Nordic introspection.

Although *Margurite's* can be classified as abstract expressionism,
there are certain references in the painting to the personal experiences
of the artist which offer an avenue of entrance for the onlooker.
Before the eye and mind can jointly go through the categories of
recognition, the painting first insists on imposing a deep sense of
coolness. With the exception of a very few touches of warm color,
the entire palette of the painter is made up of blues, blue-greens and
near-whites. After this sensation of coolness the spectator is pulled
into the picture space by the light and dark vertical thrusts from the
bottom of the painting toward the warmer areas near the center of
the painting. The space he walks through is a strange kind of dream-
like space as though he were visiting the ruins of a forgotten room
from his childhood, when he is suddenly confronted with the almost
blinding glare of a light from the upper left. As the eye becomes
adjusted the light moves in spectral shapes clockwise down to the
entering streak of light in the lower right corner. After this journey
the shapes begin to assume the aspect of form or become space with
a heavily laden air.

margurite's by William Lee Freeland. Top award in Delaware Show of Oils and Sculpture, Delaware Art Center, Wilmington, Delaware.

statement by juror

I chose William Lee Freeland's painting because it showed superior painterly qualities and was definitely in a modern direction . . . well composed and visualized with dynamic affirmation.

ADELYN D. BREESKIN, Foreman

jurors

Adelyn Breeskin, Director, Baltimore Museum of Art, Baltimore, Maryland; Frank Kleinholz, Port Washington, New York; Jack Tworkov, Pratt Institute, New York.

frank gunter

Mr. Gunter is now teaching Art in Murray State College, Murray, Kentucky. He is listed in Who's Who in American Art.

statement by the artist

I have never been easily and quickly associated with the painting theories or approaches of any single person or group. Of course, any artist is constantly being indirectly influenced. His entire life may seem to be little more than a procession of endless influences and stimulations. But, as I matured, I realized that I no longer needed the close association or friendship of other painters in order to express my own views about painting. I now feel painting is so entirely a self-involvement that personal relationships with other artists for the purpose of esthetic completion of self are unnecessary, at least for me.

I have few really close friends. Like others, I enjoy the admiration of my associates and friends, but what they think and what I, on the other hand, think about art seldom cross in conversation. Perhaps my reluctance to discuss my paintings is simply a matter of having nothing to say about them. Why I painted a given picture is certainly of no explainable importance. What it means is a faint stir inside that I have really not pinpointed.

Annunciation was originally planned as a vertical landscape. But, as is often the case in my working process, a spark of some other idea gave rise to an entirely new problem, and I found myself with a totally different finished picture. In this case, I forgot to turn the board upright, after leaving it overnight. Only after I had become involved in vertical planes on a horizontal surface, did I remember that I had been previously dealing with just the opposite. The title stems from interest in the art of the Italian Renaissance and holds no particular religious implications.

critic's comments

In this painting the artist does not want us to see any subject matter that is directly from religious iconography. We must admit that before we knew this we were attempting to force the forms we saw on the canvas into some framework of a traditional "Annunciation". The more we forced, the more we felt the intransigent resistance of the forms to any such literal interpretation. It was true, we could see any number of faces, figures, hands, and yet throughout the process we were continuously annoyed by the feeling that we were simply distorting the painting, very much in the same way that an adult (lacking the free fancy of a child) feels when he is making images of the clouds, realizing that his intention does not make the image, nor is the image maintained by his will.

The first and most dominating of the figures is just left of center, and is emphasized by a strong three-dimensional diagonal entering the painting from its base. This form pushes the figure back into space and accommodates the rather mysteriously amorphous form on the left. The color relationships on the dominant figure, being in terms of warm and cool, emphasize the presence of light, which is repeated in an ellipse to the left of the amorphous shape, and to the right in two near-circles and less intensely in elliptical lines and shapes. The greatest feeling of depth is just to the right of center, with forms that suggest a state of becoming.

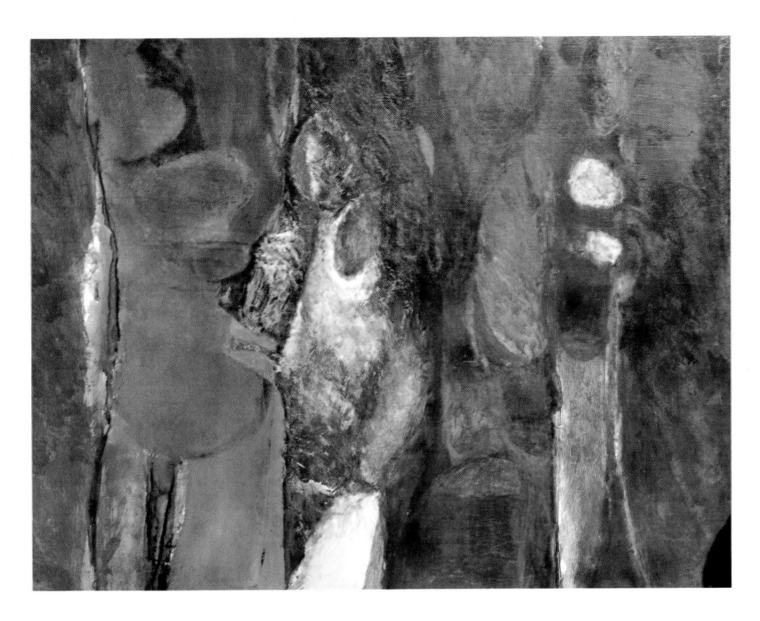

annunciation by Frank Gunter. Top award in Regional Competition, Jacksonville Art Museum, Jacksonville, Florida.

statement by critic

One of the outstanding features in this painting is the unique way in which the artist treated the hackneyed theme of the Annunciation.

judges

James Byrns, North Carolina Museum of Art, Raleigh, North Carolina; Russell Thornton, Director, Hunter Gallery, Chattanooga, Tennessee; George Kacherigis, University of North Carolina, Chapel Hill, North Carolina.

william m. halsey

Mr. Halsey is listed in Who's Who in American Art. He now lives in Charleston, South Carolina, and is frequently called on to be a juror and lecturer.

What I paint is what I am. Every painting is, in one way or another, a self-portrait. Since what I am changes from day to day, and from year to year, what I paint changes, too. I happily admit to the sin of inconsistency, and just as happily quote somebody famous who said "consistency is the hobgoblin of little minds." Nowadays, it is considered very necessary to acquire a "style", meaning a technical formula for painting. Real style comes not from a technique of painting, but from a philosophy of seeing and of living. Bonnard had real style because he had no style at all. His individuality was a result of vision, not of a clever brushstroke.

Like Adolphe Gottlieb, "I consider myself a traditionalist, but I believe in the spirit of tradition, not in the restatement of restatements." My art training was traditional, and I am glad it was. I am convinced that the best modern painters are those with traditional backgrounds. Before you can depart from anything, you must know what you are departing from.

I deplore the people who say "only realism is good" or "only abstraction is good." They are interested in fashion, not painting. I like many kinds of paintings from many ages. It is the quality of the work that counts, and the quality of the artist, not the school in which he works.

I try to paint not a description, not a picture, but an essence, the essence of a place, a feeling, a thought. To some people these essences speak; to many perhaps they do not. To some they may say other things than what they say to me. I like to feel that as I paint, the painting begins to have a life of its own; it becomes, and it demands certain things. I work with it, and I fight with it. Eventually there comes a resting place, a unity, an entity. The painting has become a thing complete on its own, inevitable.

Unlike many of my paintings, *Rocks, Sand and Sea* has a specific subject. It represents a section of the beach on Sullivan's Island near Charleston, S. C. . . . a place that I have seen for many years on summer days. A number of quick sketches, plus long familiarity with the scene, were the basis for the beginning of the painting. Its early stages were much more realistic than the final state. Edges were sharper, contours of rocks against sand, sand against sea, more defined. To many people the painting would have seemed more complete in earlier phases of its development than it does now. A picture of a particular place was not what I had in mind, however. My concern was rather with the mood of a place, the smell of rocks and hidden salty pools, the shimmer of sun on sand and water; a distillation of feeling and form, not a pictorial map of a location.

So, after having the painting in my studio for months and feeling dissatisfied with it, I finally brought myself to the point of destroying it . . . partially, at least. A lot of the detail was obliterated, nuances eliminated, color areas massed and simplified to get greater feeling of light and space. Frequently, I find that destruction is a major part of the creative process. It proved so here. The process of obliterating brought out the quality of sun-shimmer and wave-glint I had in mind . . . and the result was *Rocks, Sand and Sea* as it is today.

critic's comments

To the sailor, the lure of the sea is an old story. Like guns and ships, it is frequently referred to as feminine, perhaps because all men are essentially lonely . . . or perhaps it appears to have so many facets, all of which end up in an eternal mystery. Since the ancients put forth to sea in their frail crafts to the present time, the change has been but little. True, there are radios, larger craft, radar, and more efficient life-saving devices; but more often than not, it is still simply man and the sea. And this contrast has remained more elemental in its mystery than any other.

The composition of this painting puts the contrast quite simply. The horizon line is high to indicate the vast spread of the water. The depth of the picture space is accomplished by a reversed "z" movement. The sky is locked into the design by a light repetition of the water, and a heavier repetition of the warmth in the upper right-hand corner. The severe horizon line is in contrast to the ragged, excited line of the rocks and water in the foreground.

rocks, sand and sea by William M. Halsey. Top award in Exhibition of South Carolina Artists, Carolina Art Association, Gibbes Art Gallery, Charleston, South Carolina.

statements by the judges

The painting *Rocks, Sand and Sea* by Mr. William Halsey is a fine example of abstract design acting as structural basis for the presentation of subject matter. The artist has retained his forms as abstract entities, yet he has not sacrificed subject implication in order to produce the "academic" non-objective product which is common today. Mr. Halsey is painterly, in so far as his paint application retains the spontaneity associated with emotional reaction to color and form, and at the same time he is controlled as a composer. This balance of both emotion and intellect has established Mr. Halsey as one of the outstanding painters in the South.

CHARLES K. SIBLEY, Judge
College of William and Mary
Norfolk, Virginia

The painting *Rocks, Sand and Sea* by William Halsey demonstrates a spontaneous usage of the mixed medium. This freedom is employed with an awareness shown for pictorial values, exemplified by his total range of choice in structure, subject matter, color, etc. The sensitive balance between the demands of the picture plane and his individual manner of direction produces a personal vision.

EDWARD ROSS, Judge
Roswell, Georgia

alfred e. hammer

Mr. Hammer is now Assistant Professor of
Drawing and Painting at the Rhode
Island School of Design, Providence,
Rhode Island.

statement by the artist

My interest is mainly in the out-of-doors. I have a fond feeling
for the red barn of the Sunday painter because I know his world, and
I respect his interest as much as I deplore his lack of depth. As
a painter matures, he is apt to lose touch with his early picture-
making experiences because respect for art slowly replaces the un-
sophisticated fun of rendering red barns in blue-shadowed snow. He
loses the very thing that attracted him to painting in the first place.
A serious painter goes through an inevitable, long learning period
when fun is given over to study. Study gives substance to talent.
Without it, talent goes ballooning off to burst in thin air.

But there comes a time when the painter must ask himself why
he paints. He answers this firmly or he loses himself in superficial
current trends.

Simply to be up-to-date is one thing. To be up-to-date for a reason
is another.

I feel a strong need to recapture something of my past, to feel again
about things as I once did before I had any notion about art and
such things. One would call me a romantic, I am sure, yet there
comes a time, perhaps almost immediately, during the painting when
the material and tools assert themselves and have to be reckoned
with. This doesn't make the original aim of expressing my notions
about a place very easy.

Harbor is a real place. I didn't paint it on the spot, but I spent a
long time experiencing it. When I began to paint it, I had a very
definite idea about my awareness of this place and what I wanted to
say about it. I succeeded in my own mind. Whether my very personal
feeling is communicated to the spectator, I don't really care, nor do I
think it makes any difference. The point is that it is necessary to me.
It gets me to paint a picture, and it makes painting it worthwhile. I
feel very close to it thereafter.

critic's comments

Harbor is sonnet-like in its construction, the large left-hand area
forming the octave, the remaining right-hand section the sestet. The
entire painting has undergone a geometrical discipline, with one
visual metaphor remaining, "the clouds are crests of waves touching
the earth". Is not the air frequently described as the sea of air? Do
we not refer to planes as being ships? The diagonal which indicates
the caesura makes only a slight change in mood. The far horizon
line is a little darker, a little closer, the light a little brighter. The
large dark shape toward the lower right calls across the caesura to the
faintly nimbused rectangle in the sea, and is answered. And this
answer like a riming couplet closes the painting, for the space has
been made real.

harbor by Alfred E. Hammer. Top award in Exhibition of the Art Association of Newport, Rhode Island.

statement by juror

Our main gallery, in which Mr. Hammer's canvas was hung, is a very large room, but the strength and glow of his shapes and colors carried effectively to the least initiate eye. While these are evocative of his harbor theme, they transcend the particulars of the locale and each spectator senses the universal quality of harbors, or his own psychological harbor, in the canvas. Hammer, too, has a way of making the paint, as such, beautiful stuff.

MARION K. CARRY
Chairman of jury of hanging and awards
Annual Exhibition, Newport Art Association

jurors

Mrs. E. S. R. Brandt, Newport, Rhode Island; Francis A. Comstock, Princeton, New Jersey; William H. Drury, Newport, Rhode Island; Mrs. William H. Drury, Newport, Rhode Island; Frederick W. Goode, Atherton, California; Richard Grosvenor, St. George's School, Newport, Rhode Island; Bruce Howe, Peabody Museum, Harvard University, Cambridge, Massachusetts; Marion K. Carry, Newport, Rhode Island.

raymond han

Mr. Han is now living in New York City.

statement by the artist

It would be just about impossible for me to uncover the steps which led to *The Change*. Painting, for me, has less to do with subject matter as physical reality than with the sensual affinity that I have for any variation that arrests my fancy at the moment. My problem is to "paint this out." I may say that it is the same painting that strives to be painted time and again. The form that it takes is tentative; it is this circumstance that presents new problems and lends impetus.

critic's comments

In color, in the simplification of the forms, in the frontality of the figures and the elimination of perspective illusion, this picture is related to the contemporary Italian Metaphysical school. It is certainly refreshing, after so much insistency by the "doom" painters on our mutability, to find a picture that can insist on our animality without wallowing in it. This is satire, but very gentle satire . . . gentle but not shallow, for the ramifications are extensive. Helplessness is not confined to infancy. And how often is our celebrated rationality, that supposedly elevates us from the animal kingdom, as transparent as a diaper?

Though destined for the sightless eyes of the dead alone, the walls of the Egyptian tombs were covered with paintings celebrating the glory of life. Each civilization in its turn has celebrated some embodied conception of life in its arts, some record of its enthusiasms in nature, society, man, and God. Just as the pre-condition of living things is the apparent unilateral flow of time forming the matrix of being, so the consciousness of man in the act of selection and rejection becomes indissociable from the object of its contemplation.

But objects and relationship multiply faster than the splintering crystals of water on the rocks at the base of the falls. Image follows swiftly on image, so multifarious that it defies containment. Given the most comprehensive and inclusive enthusiasms, something remains unattended that torments like the beckoning comfort of a desert mirage by day, or the glimpse of the ephemeral dance of the will-o'-the-wisp at night.

A large portion of education consists in the conscious direction of enthusiasms, and it is through this formal and informal education that society transmits to its initiate the acceptable and the unacceptable areas of life for the exercise of enthusiasm. Most of what is transmitted consists of religious, ethical and moral judgments . . . but these judgments may be distorted beyond their intended purpose, and include for the painter not only what to see but how to see it. The *what* and *how* may be rigid as in the case of the Egyptians, or fluid and adventurous as in the case of the Renaissance.

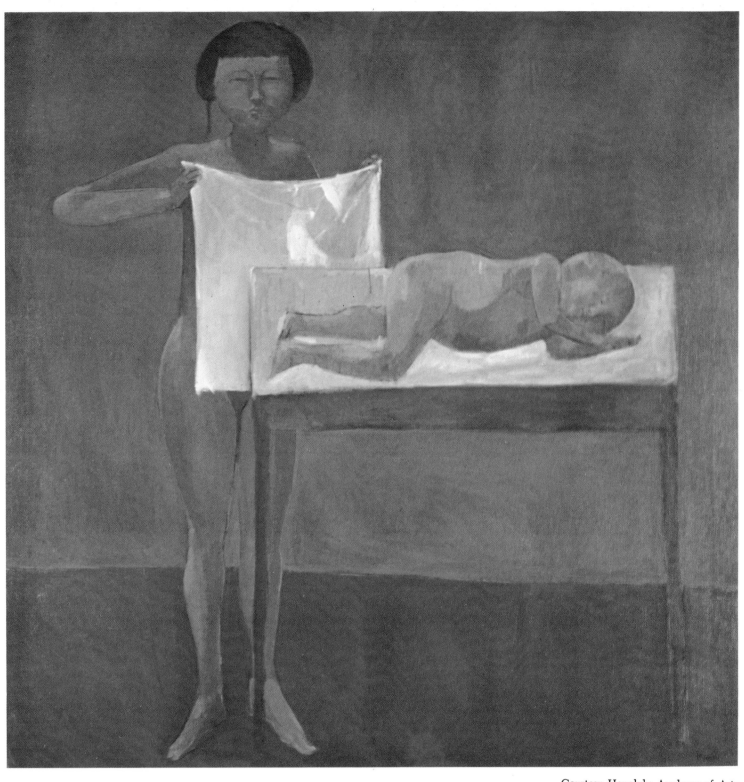

the change by Raymond Han. Top award in Artists of Hawaii, Honolulu Academy of Arts, Honolulu, Hawaii.

statement by the juror

Raymond Han is a young artist of exceptional talent who works in a realistic tradition that takes its subject matter from daily life. In *The Change*, Mr. Han shows his preoccupation with the abstract values of composition. The jury awarded this painting first prize because of its superb and subtle handling of structure, and the completeness of its conception.

KENNETH KINGREY
Associate Professor of Art
University of Hawaii

45

ceslovas janusas

Since 1958, Mr. Janusas has been the Second Vice-President of the Art League of Long Island, New York. He lives in Richmond Hill.

statement by the artist

In this painting I tried to depict the mood, the dynamic motions of sea water, and to make it rich in color. I think I did my best. That is the secret.

critic's comments

The frequency with which a question is asked, as well as the similarity of phrasing which arises from a particular taste in painting, represents a vague but constant wonder and dissatisfaction at some of the answers contemporary painting has to offer. This vague wonder and dissatisfaction is deep in the current of most lay thinking on painting. The question is usually put this way, "If the purpose of painting is to portray beauty, then why not look in Nature until you have found what is beautiful and then just sit down and paint it as it is?"

Actually the question is a rhetorical one, which takes for granted, first, that the purpose of painting is beauty (which very few will agree that it is); secondly, it assumes a theory of Nature; thirdly, that beauty is independently in Nature without a beholder; fourthly, a technique of sufficient perspicacity to record the ocular sensations. There have been, of course, experiments along these lines by people who were not totally devoid of technique, with the expected result that complete objectivity is impossible, that there is always at work, either consciously or unconsciously, the process of selection and rejection, plus the exasperating (to them at least) limitations of their vision and technique. But the motive behind even such experiments as this does not appear to be singular or simply compounded. If asked what the motive is, the reply might be, "that you could see what I saw." Where does this place the position of the picture? If this is so, then the painting is not a "mirror up to Nature", but rather a transparent glass, and the painting ceases to be a thing in itself and becomes a utilitarian vehicle for the appreciation of Nature watchers who do not have eyes of their own to see with. The direction would then be for art to send man to nature and not nature sending man to art.

Further, there is the problem of technique. With such a motive, can the technique efface itself? Will there not be the temptation for the technique to relapse into pyrotechnics for their own sake?

Here the technique reaches in two directions: (1) toward the past and the traditional emphasis on craftsmanship; (2) toward the concentration of a particular facet of the sea, wherein the totality of the elements extracted from nature become subjugated to the dominance of a moon. The warm sky sets the key which is reflected throughout the painting. Further unity is achieved by the analogies drawn between the cloud shapes and the varieties of the breakers and white caps.

ocean by Ceslovas Janusas. Top award in National Spring Exhibition, Art League of Long Island, New York.

statement by critic

The judge and jury here were probably attracted by the brilliance of color in expressing nature's marvels and the use of light to give rhythm.

jurors

Fredrick Whitaker, Foreman, Norwalk, Connecticut; Leslie Fliegel, Jackson Heights, New York; Louise Gibala, Little Neck, New York; Mable Kathryn Hatt, Douglaston, New York; William J. Witkus, Greenwich, Connecticut; Ruth Yates, New York City Center Gallery, New York.

ralph m. johnson

Mr. Johnson is now Assistant Professor of Art at the University of California, Davis, California.

statement by the artist

Painting is a means of giving visual form to ideas. These ideas seem to spring from the intellect but are formed and molded in their process of creation by experiences, perceptions, emotions and that vast, vague area known as the unconscious. Since ideas are the only things man can create, painting is tangible evidence of a basic drive to want to create. Its tangibleness seems to indicate this desire to reaffirm his own being.

I feel that it is in the realm of the unconscious that the strongest roots of painting are to be found. The origins of all things are vague, and great things are created only out of this vagueness. Refinement occurs only to that which has already been created and is a technical aspect of painting.

The artist rebels at what is known and already observed and looks to what is not; the viewer most often approaches painting looking for the opposite things. This is in answer to a question which readily comes up concerning what the contemporary painter is trying to communicate. It is not his intention or responsibility to communicate but rather to discover and to present visual ideas.

For example, the painting *Egyptian Moon* started from a rather comprehensive and representational sketch of my wife playing a grand piano. In transferring the idea from drawing to canvas, color and light became the major elements since they were more or less neglected in the drawing. They became important, first in terms of the particular scene, and later the particular aspects of subdued color and dramatic light. This led me to emphasize certain shapes, one of which had been the raised lid of the piano and finally became the "moon" shape.

I do not feel that the title is misleading since I was obviously not trying to create representational form. I think that titles have relatively little importance to the painting, and in this case, I think of it in the form of a romantic suggestion.

critic's comments

The first impression of the *Egyptian Moon* is one of a painting, two-dimensional in its space, decorative in its intention, with some textural differentiation in its areas.

This impression does not last, for areas begin to advance and recede according to the color surrounding them. Thus the semicircle of blue in the right half of the picture seems to be applied on top of the brown. The yellow rectangle at the bottom of the picture, because it is placed next to the blue which is its near-complement, tends to form a receding plane leading to the brown area. A definite ocular resistance is felt when the eye tries to force the upper red rectangle to move toward the right blue semicircle, for the red rectangle moves up to the top of the picture and is stopped by a line moving into the upper yellow sector. Three black accents accelerate the movement of the swinging yellow arc in its trip to pick up the line of the right blue area. The movement is reversed by the convergence of the black line through the brown area at the base of the blue semicircle.

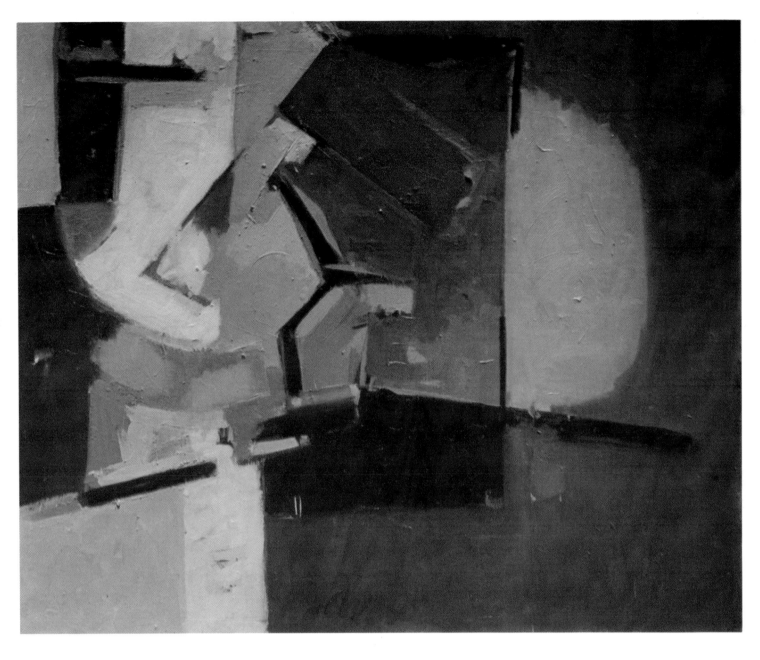

egyptian moon by Ralph M. Johnson. Top award winner in the California State Fair and Exposition, Sacramento, California.

statement by critic

The exciting elements in this painting are its balance and construction . . . and the broad execution employed by the artist.

jurors

Maria Von Ridelstein, San Francisco, California; Lenard Kester, Los Angeles, California; Joe Waano-Gano, Los Angeles, California; Fritz Kocher, Los Angeles, California; Keith Crown, Manhattan Beach, California, Associate Prof. of Fine Arts, University of Southern California, Los Angeles, Calif.; Karl Kasten, Lafayette, California, Professor of Art, University of California, Berkeley, California.

lucien kapp

Mr. Kapp is now painting
in Decatur, Illinois.

statement by the artist

Art is a narrow truth. A vast continuum seeking its own image. I paint within the limitations of the prevailing mode. Its time in the continuum seems right.

The *Yoshiwara-Camphor Light* was painted in 1959 during my last year of graduate work at the University of Illinois. I had recently returned from Navy duty in the Far East aboard a supply ship home-ported in Yokosuka, Japan. The experience modified my entire perceptual structure. Another event was to modify it further. Lawrence Calcagno came to the University that year as visiting artist. So much should be said. How intense the response to creative necessity. How complete the commitment. The prints and words of Lee Chesney comprise another vital influence. My painting at that time reflects an attempt at synthesis with these forces. The process continues with a measure of self-identity.

I saw the Yoshiwara area of Tokyo during early evening rain. I did not seek ancient Edo in neon arcs. There were no stolid courtesans of Utamaro in the fade damp. Only bars, brothels . . . blazing echo light . . . lonely.

critic's comments

There is a tendency in criticism today to measure the importance of a painting in terms of its influence on contemporaries as well as subsequent painters . . . the reason being that it throws light upon the so-called "style of the times."

In contrast to this there are masters and master works that appear to be either outside "the style of the times" or to inspire no adherents to their departure among their fellow artists. They are regarded as a self-contained terminus outside the flow of tradition. Influential importance may never come in later generations, but when and if the influence does occur, it does so in a way that may be highly deceptive and difficult to discern, for it almost invariably involves the use of the plastic means rather than an obvious mannerism. This difficulty arises because the plastic means may be in opposition to the influence: instead of smooth-flowing, graceful lines, adhering to the surface of the painting, they may be rough, disrupted and bold; through contrasts of color and value and linear direction, the kind of picture space may change: the palette may go from a bright, happy key to a dull, somber one. Obviously the painter using this kind of influence (and very few painters have not) is making the assertion that the value of the picture is not to be found in its social milieu, but rather in the being of the painting itself.

Although Yoshiwara-Camphor Light is a figurative painting, the linear excitement is equal to some examples of the non-figurative type, for in this case the line is fulfilling other functions than itself. For a moment of perception it may describe a tree branch, suddenly become interrupted and delineate mass, only to dive into deeper space and emerge again. The reticence in the use of color produces the sensation of moonlight. Had there been a greater domination of the picture by the light areas, the effect would have been one of the intense noon-day sun. At a distance the landscape is clearly seen. But as one approaches nearer, the painting becomes a kind of picture writing.

yoshiwara–camphor light by Lucien Kapp. Top award winner in the Central Illinois Exhibition, Decatur Art Museum, Decatur, Illinois.

statement by the judge

Mr. Kapp's painting was chosen for first prize because it was an outstanding painting in a contemporary technique of a sensitively realized landscape scene. The painting showed good technical training in the art of painting itself (that is, preparation of canvas, knowledge of painting) and an assimilated knowledge of painting techniques of the second half of the century. Mr. Kapp has a positive image to project in this painting.

WILLIAM N. EISENDRATH, JR.
Assistant Director
City Art Museum of St. Louis

m. j. kitzman

Mr. Kitzman is now painting in Cedar Falls, Iowa.

statement by the artist

Painting is a graphic communication of the artist's inner subjective vision. It is the sum of his sensory perceptions. Perception takes place behind the eye. I have no verbal message to add to the message of my paintings. They are intended to be objective enough to speak for themselves and subjective enough to stimulate and heighten the aesthetic perception of the viewer.

Painting is a continuous activity. For me it is contingent upon my experiences, fantasies, dreams, conscious and subconscious. A painting is realized through the process, not entirely premeditated, yet not left to accident or intuitive action process.

The painting *White Table: Still Life* is one of many paintings involving the still life theme, a favorite of mine. As to a statement about the steps leading to the painting of this specific work, I can say nothing more than it was an effort on my part to paint a good painting.

I am a young artist (30), and I tire of young artists trying to make profound statements about their work. I do not understand the reasons for painting. I know it is good for me to paint, and I am gratified if someone else finds something of joy in my painting.

critic's comments

Those who knew the working methods of Cezanne tell us that before he painted a still life he thoughtfully considered the position of each object, carefully arranging them until they satisfied his demands. In most art schools this procedure is still carried out; and contained in each still life arrangement is some pre-considered problem that the teacher wishes the student to solve. This is not without its pedagogical dangers, for alas, most of us are all too familiar with the wrung-dry, embalmed results; and indeed it would be ridiculous to point to Cezanne as the founding father of this oh-so-still, still lifes.

There are others who feel that the plastic problems of still life become more real if they are not so consciously arranged . . . in a phrase, if the objects become the passive recipients of the life around them. *White Table: Still Life* belongs to this order, if we extend this order to mean that the temporal element is also considered, for this is a still life coming into being. A large, not so white, but pink table, one that might be found in most kitchens, is the dramatic framework for the still life to take place. It is surrounded by a dark pattern which at intervals is differentiated to indicate space. The still life that is intruding on the table's space is moving down from the upper right portion of the picture. The tension between the variations on the left side of the table top and an implied equilateral triangle off right center continues to pull the still life into the table space.

white table: still life by M. J. Kitzman. Top award in Exhibition of Sioux City Art Center, Sioux City, Iowa.

statement by critic

The shocking technique . . . rather than the subject matter . . . probably captivated the judge's favor toward this painting.

jury

Mr. Robert O. Hodgell, Art Director, Extension Division, University of Wisconsin.

fred
kline

Since 1955, Mr. Kline has been teaching painting and teacher training classes at the Toledo Museum of Art, Toledo, Ohio.

statement by the artist

My painting *Night* is a painting about feelings. But it is not the record of my feelings about a particular place or moment in my life. Rather it is an accumulation of all the things I have seen, abstracted and organized to express all I have ever felt and learned, all that I am. I learn much from nature, and here I have tried to show man's oneness with nature.

I believe that art is created by the subconscious or innermost part of man. If words could express the whole meaning of a painting, it would be a shallow and meaningless work of art, for words tell no more than the rational mind sees. One cannot verbalize about the subconscious meaning of a painting, about the deep chords of emotion it strikes within one, which are the most important part of it. So it is necessary for the observer to look at a painting with his heart or soul and not merely with his eyes and mind, for if he does use only his eyes and mind, he will see no more than the superficialities. Meaningful art speaks through the soul or heart and uses the eyes and mind only as instruments of communication.

critic's comments

After the initial impact of a painting is stored away in the past of the perceiver's mind, it does not remain there idly, but becomes a dynamic center of force, pulling all relevant experiences into it as well as casting off all those associations which are irrelevant. This process, not unlike the selections and rejections which go on in the artist's mind while painting, may stimulate the mind into speculation as to how this painting came about through all the maze of choices, decisions and parturitions.

If a painter only paints his complete works, then the totality would present concrete evidence of this psychical process in material form.

In studying this painting, three names come to mind . . . Albert Pinkham Ryder, Ferdinand Hodler, and Marsden Hartley . . . the reason being that all three of these painters used clouds with a nimbus of light as natural nocturnal symbols. All three of the painters as well as the canvas we are viewing were either thoroughly engrossed in mysticism or at least touched by it. Ryder referred to the nature in painting as being a new creation . . . Hodler an intensification by repetition . . . and Hartley, that painting as well as nature is an intellectual idea. The latter statement may be just another way of saying that there are allegorical functions in painting that are inescapable; and it is interesting to note that none of the three escaped allegory.

Concerning *Night*, with its emphasis on mysticism, with no allegory, we wonder if the artist has escaped, or if the future may contain a new "Temple of the Mind."

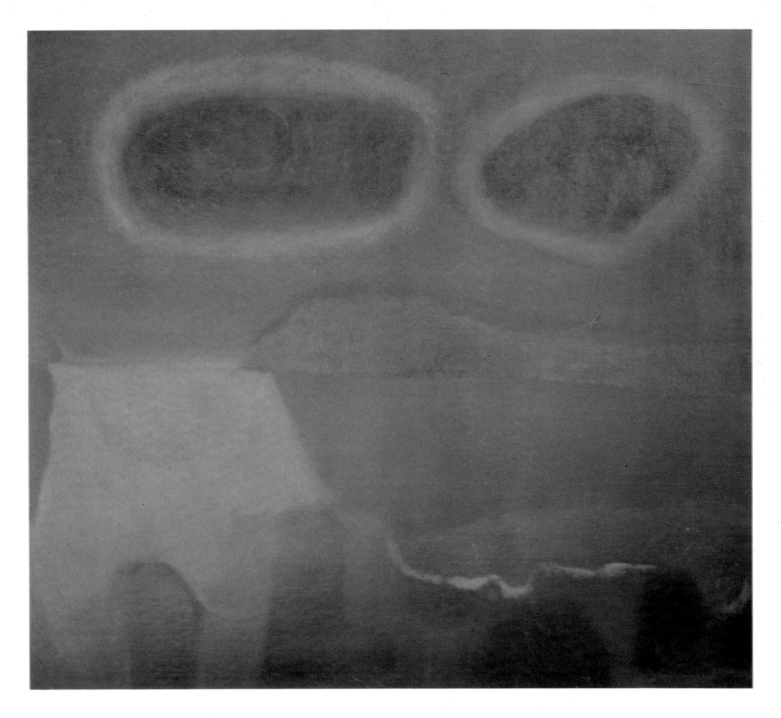

night by Fred Kline. Top award winner in the Exhibition of Toledo Area Artists, Toledo Museum of Art, Toledo, Ohio.

statement by critic

Analyze the excellent use of a single color in this monochromatic composition, and you'll see why the judge was probably drawn to this painting.

judges

Emerson Burkhart, Painter; Daniel Rhodes, State University of New York; Allen S. Weller, University of Illinois.

gerd koch

Mr. Koch is currently teaching Art History at Ventura College, California, and teaches private students and conducts seminars at various art clubs and associations. He is listed in Who's Who in American Art.

I lived till my 22nd year in Detroit, a large city atmosphere, but I have always had a strong interest in the beauty of nature. This seems to have arisen from extensive travel to spots of dramatic natural beauty. I remember camping at first in my very young years and a trip to Germany at 6 years . . . the walks through the forest, the Rhine, and the castles are still vivid in my mind. Then the family went farther in automobile tours and finally I was off on my own on bicycle, hiking, and canoeing trips with the American Youth Hostel group as a leader or with three or four friends.

This slow and thoughtful mode of travel intensified my stimulation by, and feeling of oneness with nature. Up to this time my photography, still and movie, was sufficient to record these moods. But moving to California by way of a three months' painting tour of the West started the need for self-expression.

First, a short sojourn on a coastly mountain pass overlooking the San Ynez Valley, then six months on a small valley ranch culminated finally in our own two acres in the Ojai Valley covered with native plants of the chapparal, oak, and olive trees.

Gradually, I realized my feelings of nature in my painting, after four series that dealt with different aspects of nature . . . the cycles of the seasons and the times of the day, paintings of the browns and yellows of California summers and falls, winter with storm clouds over the mountains . . . the rich color during and after a rain (it only rains in the winter and spring in California). These were paintings of inward vision, abstractions that began and left some of the objects surrounded by the all powerful force . . . time.

This painting was conceived finally last spring when greens of new growth (leaves, wild flowers) broke forth. I began to paint in pure colors. I have nearly always painted outdoors, direct from the scene, moving from spot to spot seeking light, structure and mood that for me gives the object its strongest beauty. I do many color drawings and large and small oil and casein paintings that repeat and experiment with the themes.

Spring Garden with Sun Wet Path developed from the strong contrast of sun-lit areas and deep shade. The sun, high and beyond the trees, is stark white on the path. A few flowers among the native plants and the trees on the side and in back are in deep shadow, thus becoming solid mass. Calligraphy of vigorous brush strokes are lines of growth . . . strength within, and some the light on leaves and stems. The *TIME* . . . the surging force of trooping quail, streaming ants, and the droppings of the plants are just part of the unspoken urgency of nature.

COLOR PHOTO BY BRUCE HOWELL
COURTESY LOS ANGELES COUNTY MUSEUM OF HISTORY, SCIENCE AND ART, EXPOSITION PARK

spring garden with sun wet path by Gerd Koch. Top award in Exhibition of Artists of Los Angeles and Vicinity, Los Angeles County Museum of History, Science and Art, Los Angeles, California.

statements by judges

". . . several slow trips around the galleries gradually bring out those works which sustain one's interest and invite repeated and increasingly enjoyable inspection. A sparkling landscape by Gerd Koch certainly deserved the double accolade it received in winning a major prize and a purchase award."

HENRY J. SELDIS
Los Angeles Times

"In the largest media area, oil painting . . . to my eyes there are many clear standouts. Among them are . . . the gay activity of the prize-winning *Spring Garden* . . . by Gerd Koch."

CHARLENE COLE
Beverly Hills Times

"By and large, the show favors spontaneous, free-wheeling abstractions. . . . No question, the exhibition is a lively affair, bursting out all over with exuberant, high-keyed, unrestrained color.

Among the better known "names" . . . Gerd Koch . . . is represented with top-notch examples."

JULES LANGSNER
Art News

judges

Elmer Bischoff, Chairman Fine Arts Dept., California School of Fine Arts, San Francisco, Painter; Kenneth B. Sawyer, Art Critic; David Smith, Sculptor, Bolton Landing, N. Y.; Henry J. Seldis, *Los Angeles Times*; Charlene Cole, *Beverly Hills Times*; Jules Langsner, *Art News*.

ida kohlmeyer

Since 1957, Miss Kohlmeyer has been on the faculty of the Newcomb Art Department of Tulane University, where she teaches drawing and painting.

statement by the artist

The act of painting, to me, is a celebration . . . not that it is always pleasurable . . . in fact, it seldom is. But it is, or should be, liberation from restrictions and prejudices, in the sense that all decisions rest in my hands. I am answerable to myself, alone. Since I hold that I am my sole judge, the painting becomes an act of integrity, not convention.

Heretofore, painting served as a servant to tradition, to the rich, or to the spiritual, as in church art. Now it has become spirit itself. Consequently, much of contemporary art is emotional, highly introspective at times, lyrical at others, and largely non-representational. This turn to non-objectivity could well be due in part to the artist's desire to improve upon the world as he finds it.

I dream of a world of harmony enlivened by the spirit of adventure and freedom of choice, a world in which painting does not "contradict itself as painting no matter how successful it may be as illustration." * I do not feel it necessary to depict a saint or a martyr to invoke a spiritual atmosphere. This must happen through bare means . . . no props, no haloes, no burning bush . . . merely through intensity of purpose, brush and paint. Which is more real, the flower we see or the anguish we feel? The tree, or fear? We owe the misconception that art is a combination of skill, techniques, and representation to the ideals of the Renaissance. Art became literary, and remained so until today.

". . . a kind of spirit language with universal human meanings that go far beyond the limits of the concrete and the particular . . . which crosses all superficial boundaries of language, nationality, and time." ** It transcends change. A painting should be an invention, not an imitation . . . a reflection of the times, and prophetic of things to come. This can only come about in a rarified atmosphere of the highest state of sensitivity attainable by man. It is this state which is beautiful, and the beauty is magically conveyed through the work of art.

I am involved in a search for this kind of beauty. For a long time, I looked for it in symbolism. My quest now is with the metaphysical. My painting must contain the dichotomies which make up life itself. I experience these oppositions at every turn . . . moments of revelation and despair, of ecstacy and disillusion. To be alive presupposes the ability to withstand such contrasts, tensions, stresses. These are the objects I deal with in my work . . . rather than with the changeable and untrustworthy objects I see.

I am asked what steps led to the painting of *Transverse.* My whole life has been a preparation for this act, as my whole life has been responsible for any decision I have ever made.

critic's comments

For some time now it has become quite evident that the reduction of the plastic relationships employed by Mondrian was not sufficient

---

* Statement by Ray Parker: *It Is* Magazine, 2nd Edition.
** *The New Art Education,* by Ralph M. Pearson, page 43.

transverse by Ida Kohlmeyer. Top award in *Southwest American Painting Exhibition, Oklahoma Art Center, Oklahoma City, Oklahoma.*

to the Modern School in defining the limits of painting, or a field which specifically belonged to painting. In Mondrian's last canvasses there still remained allusions to the world, and if not the visible world to the world of conception. This, by some, was considered to be a lack of purity, a point of reference which was outside the realm of the primary purpose of painting, which they insisted must become itself.

This argument is seen much more easily in the realm of music. A note from an oboe does not represent anything except itself. A symphony generally does not try to reproduce the sounds heard in nature. So why should a color put down on canvass be compelled to have a reference to some natural image? Why should lines be forced to be descriptive?

These are some of the questions that we feel the painting, *Transverse,* is asking. The paint is thinned sufficiently to re-

veal the brush work and its own materiality. The color is itself and does not attempt to create any allusive images or descriptions. Have we then reached in this type of painting what belongs exclusively to concrete painting? How decisive can these limits be?

statement by critic

The judge probably felt strongly in favor of this composition because of the painter's unique way of gaining rhythm through the use of color.

judge

Gordon Bailey Washburn, Director, Department of Fine Arts, Carnegie Institute.

paul lauritz

Mr. Lauritz now devotes his time to the painting of landscapes and marines of the West. He lives in Los Angeles, California, and is listed in Who's Who in American Art.

statement by the artist

I always enjoy the solitude and quiet of hills and valleys. And in *California Hills* I was attracted to the simple composition and design, besides an interesting sky illuminating the whole landscape. It was painted in early fall. After a few showers, the hills will turn from brown to green.

Nature has always been my model. I do not copy nature, but I borrow and compose to make an interesting design. As to color, I use my own ideas. Though I experiment a good deal, I am not interested in the "isms" of today. I feel that a painting must have recognizable objects. An artist, however, must take any liberty and be free to paint as he wishes.

My philosophy is rather simple. I let nature be my guide.

critic's comments

If one had to choose one word to characterize the qualities of this landscape, the one that would occur most frequently would be "restraint". In this age of anxiety, agony, fear, and violently introspective expressionism, this kind of painting runs the risk of getting trampled under foot by the mad rush of the self-expression school to the freedom camp.

But freedom, as we know, is a hard-bought thing, and consists in more than swapping one set of prejudices for another set just because they may appear to be more shocking as conversation pieces.

To become a partisan of any school without a sincere and dedicated attempt to understand the intention and implication not only of the act of painting but the pictures themselves is sheer foolishness. Nor is this meant to condone mealy-mouthed ambiguities in accepting everything that is set to canvas as therefore good, nor the tired pseudo-sophisticate whose jaded appetites have been so surfeited that he cannot disturb his languor by the possibility that something good could come out of Nazareth.

If we are to have a true Renaissance in America, it will arise from that understanding of what binds all painting together, from the wildest to the calmest. There is no painting that does not have some abstract substructure (no matter how representational), and there is no abstraction that can be completely free from some representational inferences. If this is true, the difference is a matter of degree, not of kind, and therefore is thoroughly unsuitable as a basis of judgment one way or the other.

In *California Hills* the abstract substructure becomes the means whereby the painter utilizes the total surface of the picture plane, causing the eye of the beholder to move throughout the entire landscape. The beholder's eye moves, but he is probably unconscious of the movement as well as the reason for it, for to the realist if the *means* of movement become too obvious, they lose their function and become the *object* of awareness.

california hills by Paul Lauritz. Top award in West Coast Oil Painting Exhibition, Charles and Emma Fry Museum, Seattle, Washington.

statement by critic

The exceptional qualities in this painting are the purity of the landscape and the freshness and vivacity of the color.

judge

Adolf Dehn, Painter, New York City.

leo leibsohn

Mr. Leibsohn is currently living in Los Angeles, California.

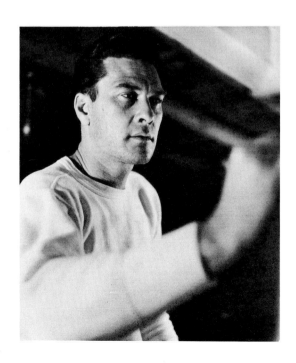

statement by the artist

I can say nothing of the "Why" of painting. That I must leave to estheticians. I can only speak of the "How" . . . and then not too well because I know so little of the motivating factors.

The source of my painting is the sum total of my experience, both conscious and unconscious. My unconscious makes marks on the canvas which my conscious either rejects through erasure, or if potentially satisfying, lets remain. The painting results not so much from intuitive action but rather as a reaction to it.

I must discover beauty, react to it, and then somehow reflect it. The reflection, which in this case is called "Still Life #2", is nothing more than a mirror with the painter standing before it. Whether the painting is significant or not, depends not on the mirror but on that which it is reflecting.

The painting reproduced here is the second of a series that has grown to considerable number.

critic's comments

From the point of view of subject matter, still life offers greater possibilities of exploration of shape and color than either the figure or the landscape. The drawing, color, and space can vary at the painter's discretion. The painting will remain a still life, and the objects will maintain something of their identity. No one is too disturbed by the liberties taken.

Not so with the human figure. Witness Gertrude Stein's remark concerning Picasso's *Three Musicians* . . . "it is a still life". *Nude Descending a Staircase* is more a study of movements and planes than it is of a human body. This, then, is one of the results of excessive reduction of the figure.

One device in modern painting which the layman may find disturbing is the importance placed on the intervals between objects. These intervals may be referred to as negative space. In this painting, however, the negative spaces have the power of becoming positive, though it is impossible to see them as positive and negative simultaneously. On examination they will be one or the other.

Many distinctions have been made concerning the use of line in painting and its influence on space and color. In this painting two types of line are used that are often considered to be mutually exclusive: where the line is sharp there is a crystalline separation of the forms, where the line diminishes and is lost as an edge the form begins to exist in a color tonality of atmosphere all its own. Because of this distinction's moving throughout the painting, and the subtly graduated architectural shapes that advance and recede in reference to the frontal plane, the entire painting assumes the character of a composite image of bottles and buildings as though reflected in a glass.

still life no. 2 by Leo Leibsohn. Top award in Southwest Artists' Exhibition, Museum of New Mexico Art Gallery, Santa Fe, New Mexico.

statement by critic

One has only to observe the rather convincing ensemble of form and color in this painting to see why it won the award.

judges

Andrew Dasburg, Ranchos de Taos, New Mexico; Vance Kirkland, Denver University; Everett Spruce, University of Texas.

charles littler

Mr. Littler is presently teaching at the University of Arizona, Tucson, Arizona.

statement by the artist

I work within the same general esthetic as most other young painters. Backgrounds, influences and temperaments vary widely, but our iconography is beginning to consolidate. The painters of the fifties . . . Gorky, DeKooning, Pollock, Rothko, Kline, etc. . . . have laid a powerful and indispensable groundwork. This has been an exciting period of revolt and discovery. I sometimes wish I could have been a part of it. They have unquestionably won their victory, and now we who are coming into maturity are obliged to strengthen and build further from their achievement. In examining our position, we have re-evaluated the contribution of other Americans who have moved outside the main direction. With men like Marin, Hofmann, Waugh, Hopper, Levine, we recognize a kinship.

I spend most of my time drawing or sketching until I can't stand any more. Then I paint. I don't make any connection between the drawings and paintings until afterward, when I see all kinds of inter-relationships. Then I start the cycle over again.

This painting, *Landscape Without Figure*, has the usual history. It reflects my experience of the desert, for which I hold mixed feelings. The desert is the most paradoxical of all landscape, and that is one reason why it keeps renewing my interest and appreciation. The desert is no better subject than any other. It just happens to absorb me, and furnishes me an external discipline I find I need to work with complete conviction.

critic's comments

The top half of this composition is conceived as an almost static blue plane, which, if necessary, may be thought of as sky, while the lower half is excited by complementary color becoming shapes that result from violent calligraphy. The lower section is again divided into half by the right edge of a cylinder, the axis of which generates an over-all, counter-clockwise movement which forces the right-hand configurations of the landscape away from the spectator, and advances the lower left-hand section, which is arrested in its movement by two diagonal lines and the black drawing over the lower yellow area. This movement is further arrested by the implied line created by the repetition of near-circular shapes which move in an elliptical pattern and find their climax at the junction of the blue-yellow contrast at the bottom of the painting.

The layman may well object that this is not *what* he sees when he is enjoying his favorite view or prospect, nor is it what he sees when he is relaxing in front of a landscape by an old master. What is most often overlooked is the previous conditioning of what he sees in Nature by how the old masters saw and interpreted the landscape in front of them. The "how" we see was used by the old masters to fortify the sense of reality of the objects presented.

This contemporary painting reverses the procedure. The "how" we see has become the subject of the painting. In nature, movement, animate or inanimate, conveys the urge to change and is opposed to solidity. Permitting the movement of line to create the solids is a contemporary answer to the older means of chiaroscuro.

landscape without figure by Charles Littler. Top award in Annual Festival Art Show, Tucson, Arizona.

statement by the judge

Landscape Without Figure by Mr. Charles Littler was chosen as winner of the Annual Festival Art Show for qualities which particularly appealed to me: a feeling of concentration matched with the artist's sensibility and response to color.

FREDRIC S. WIGHT
Director of UCLA Art Galleries
Los Angeles, California

katy madsen

Since 1958, Mrs. Madsen has been teaching Art classes for the Adult Education Program in Walnut Creek, California.

statement by the artist

I feel that a painting should tell a story or give a message. The more beautifully and interestingly it is told, the better the painting.

Pure abstract doesn't tell a story even though it may have design, color, texture, etc. It leaves almost everything up to the viewer's imagination. To me, that is no different from seeing pictures in clouds or in water stains on walls, etc. An artist should do more than that to guide the viewer. That doesn't mean he has to tell the whole story. He should leave something unsaid, or the viewer will be bored. A few lost areas and areas not tightly painted will help.

I have been interested in and have primarily painted portraits. Each person I paint is my story. The likeness and expression through good drawing is most important, and the paint has to be applied so that it is realistic though not photographic.

Before my *Lady in Black* was born, I was confronted with a woman who had lived three score or more years. Her beauty was different from youth, but to me was even more striking. My job as an artist was to get this woman and something of her life and character on canvas.

Her black dress and grey hair enhanced the color of her skin. I could and did use all the colors on my palette. Since her skin was no longer smooth, I could use loose strokes of different color and thus show her age subtly.

I liked my subject from the very beginning, but with all my subjects, I become more and more fascinated as I work. The colors seem to change before my eyes, and I try to put them all down. Even though her hair was grey, it picked up more color than it would have, had it retained its original pigment.

Her hands resting on her lap showed her character as much as her face. I could use broken color and lost-and-found edges to advantage there, to show her age and that most of her hard work was over. They were so interesting, I had to be careful not to overplay them, because I had to keep her face as the center of interest.

I will not go further with techniques or methods, but the more one paints, the more one sees that paintings can be improved upon forever. I will paint many more paintings and hope to tell the story with each one carefully, but still leave something for my viewers to add to it.

critic's comments

In Mrs. Madsen's portrait there is a balance struck between the demands of composition and likeness. The composition is based on a triangle formed by the head and the hands, a composition which has been a tradition in portrait painting since the Renaissance, not only because it enables the eye to explore all the painting but because it lends dignity and solidity to the sitter. Rather than using a black pigment for the dress, the artist has chosen a dark blue which, in the presence of the green background, gives the appearance of black. This device prevents the excessive contrast of the dress from pushing the figure into the background, as possibly would have occurred if black had been used instead.

lady in black by Katy Madsen. Top award in Statewide Art Exhibition, Santa Cruz, California.

statement by juror

"The painting . . . received first award not only for its technical excellence but for catching that elusive something (call it atmosphere or feeling) that a jury always looks for in addition to the technical skills that govern good painting. . . ." CECIL CHAMBERLIN

jurors

Cecil Chamberlin, Chairman, Los Gatos, California; Harold Ward, Sacramento, California; Louise Cunningham, Felton, California.

robert e. marx

Mr. Marx is now Professor of Fine Arts in Syracuse University. He is listed in Who's Who in American Art.

statement by the artist

An unnumbered sequence of an artist's work is important to trace the development of an idea. A specific painting in the sequence is essential for itself as well as for the context. The painting which is the inquiry . . . the seed . . . has no less value than the ensuing developmental paintings or the ultimate summation. In reality, all are variations on a theme.

The total of nature is a generality. A landscape is a specific part of this generality and is translatable in the visual terms of images and symbols. These symbols need not be real in the sense of being recognizable but should necessarily be abstract with an underlying probable realness, for the visual language expressed in symbols . . . visual parables . . . move toward and away from identifying reality.

This painting has a specific title, *Falling Water Pool*, which is precise and remote. The theme is landscape, a small part of landscape, and is a visualization of a pool and of water and of falling water; all landscape and all one. Symbols to convey these impressions are taken from a remembered past brought into the present by a thought, a remembrance, or possibly an action. The grouping and placing of these symbols and their further development, then, is the activity of painting. And in the painting the symbols changed and evolved until they served to suggest the feeling of landscape.

In no way does a painting compete with or mirror nature. Indeed, it must not, for the artist is a maker of symbols and a teller of tales. He puts on canvas, not the world that exists but the unarticulated meanings that man gives the world. However, the artist's light hand on visual reality is crucial, for the role of the symbol parallels the range of man's capacity to abstract. And this capacity and need to abstract allows him to derive common responses from the painted generality of nature and the real entity of nature. It also allows him to recognize a subtlety of statement which can be more meaningful than a correct report, and leaves open interpretations which man requires for aesthetic fulfillment.

critic's comments

To the Rationalist the horizon lines offered a definite point of reference to the position of the beholder, scattering the hierarchic implications of the Middle Ages to the winds. The enthronement of reason by the humanists had given man an assured place in the total scheme of things, and Nature became a knowable order. Nature, that is, in its more placid moments, for there are those strange drawings by Leonardo in Windsor Castle picturing the Deluge wherein the horizon line disappears behind the conical swirls of torrential rain and wind. Sheets of cataracts are frozen before the astonished gaze of the curious.

These various characteristics of water, its color, movement, reflectivity, its creativity and destructiveness have occupied the abilities of some of the greatest painting minds in the world, both Oriental and Occidental.

All too frequently we permit some suggested pre-conception to dictate what we should be seeing in a painting. And the more we try to force this image on the painting, the more the actual painting stub-

falling water pool by Robert E. Marx. Top award winner in the Exhibition of Artists of Central New York, Munson-Williams-Proctor Institute, Utica, New York.

bornly resists. This is the case with *Falling Water Pool*. A cursory glance reveals the picture as interlocking light and dark shapes held in tension in space by two "Y" shapes, three implied circles, a blue rectangle, and an unrepeated red. If one goes no further than this, it is tantamount to equating the price of admission as an index to the quality of the show.

On further examination, the entire upper shape assumes the qualities of roof tops in the rain, the reflective wetness of which is undeniable. The "Y" shapes support the appearance of tin roof tops, swallowed and ill-defined in the falling drizzle. Below the blue building and to the front of the red, the water reaches the climax of its wetness and reflects its source.

statement by judge

Robert Marx has a very deep concern with the essential structure and meaning of the subject matter in his painting.

It is a concern with structure more as it is felt than as it is visualized. To express an outward form in painting is a matter of technical proficiency. But to be able to create the inner and immediately grasped meaning of structure is an insight to which Mr. Marx is sensitive.

Falling Water Pool is a highly evocative work which presents the viewer with the essential poetry expressed in its title. It is a moment of movement, capturing the mysteries that one might find in these elements.

WILLIAM HULL, Director
Syracuse Museum of Fine Arts

judges

William E. Hull, Director, Syracuse Museum of Fine Arts; Dorothy C. Miller, Curator of the Museum Collections, Museum of Modern Art, New York City; Robert R. Vickrey, Artist, Midtown Galleries, New York City.

69

william lee moreland

Since 1955, Mr. Moreland has been Assistant Professor of Art, Department of Art and Architecture, Southwest Louisiana Institute, Lafayette, Louisiana.

statement by the artist

I am not a realist, but if I lose touch with subject I wither. The painting devices which I employ, the remaking of forms which I do, are directed toward an intense realization of the subject . . . on my own terms. But my terms are limited by the objective meaning of the subject. If I paint a *PIETA*, a dead Christ, it is the dead Christ which I must realize. I do not work away from the subject, manipulate it freely and transform it completely into a totally new thing. It is the privilege of painting to do just that, to tear the subject apart, and from its dismemberment give birth to something new. Although my painting technique is a process of search and dismemberment and destruction, I am never able to really destroy the subject. It may elude me, I may violate it or find those new things in it, but in the end I am its captive. I find the subject remains intact, in spite of being forced into my personal painting style.

I suppose this subject matter which is the source and the central concern of my painting consists largely of the human figure, in which I seem to find a potential transcendency, which I cannot really explain, but only experience in terms of the visual. It has nothing to do with beliefs or philosophies but only with direct, deep and formless feeling, to which I can give form and meaning only by the process of realization we call painting.

critic's comments

During the high Renaissance, the "Pieta" or mourning the dead Christ, which during the low Renaissance had become such a center of focus for the pouring out of human grief at the sight of the tragically mutilated body of Our Lord, became a stereotyped triangular composition which in a great many instances was simply an excuse for a nude figure, and for the most part devoid of religious feeling or artistic significance . . . in short, empty of everything except sheer physical skill.

For its compositional type, this particular "Pieta" goes back to a specific Byzantine icon type depicting the "Death of the Blessed Virgin," with its geometrical insistence of opposing verticals and horizontals. This geometrical insistence may recall cubism. If so, it would be the later, synthetic cubism, which introduced simultaneous images, such as one sees here in the movements of the three vertical figures. Here there is no interest in the nude as such. Rather, the emphasis has been placed on the sensuousness of paint and its variations as a material. Harmonically, the color is reminiscent, and appropriately so, of the Faiyum mummy portraits.

When one thinks of the acres of endless, sickly drivel that is being foisted off as religious art on a gullible public that thinks it knows what it likes, the dignity, restraint and personal conviction of this painting comes as a most welcome relief. Rather than giving the public an image to which it can rise in spirit, the pseudo-religious sells a professional fiction which lends an odor of sanctity to the dollar bill. When this saccharine fiction loses its sweetness and turns bitter to the taste, when faith is lost and disillusionment sets in because it is misdirected, the perpetrators of the fiction would crucify the Third Person of the Trinity to justify themselves, if they could find Him.

pieta by William Lee Moreland. Top award in Louisiana State Art Commission Galleries, Baton Rouge, Louisiana

statement by the foreman of the jury

I voted to give the first prize to the *PIETA* by William L. Moreland because I liked the composition and technique. The painting was dramatic and had considerable emotional impact.

Mrs. Louise B. Clark, Director
Brooks Memorial Art Gallery
Memphis, Tennessee

jurors

Mrs. Louise B. Clark, Brooks Gallery, Memphis, Tennessee; Ralph B. Hutson, Mississippi Southern College for Women, Columbus, Mississippi.

71

karla moss

Miss Moss is now painting at her home at White Gate Ranch, Stinson Beach, California.

statement by the artist

When I look at a painting, I want to see the soul as it is, alone and lonely with aching parts and ugly fears. I want to feel the quiet places where things fly away from it all, and meditate sleepily. I want to perceive ideas of the human mind . . . clever and imaginative, and the belly of guts held in, yet helplessly pouring out . . . because the effort shows. To me, the beautiful is the dignity of non-perfection . . . and the lie of perfection.

I cannot call myself an action painter because sweeping and wild strokes of luck are not enough. There are days when I am also exhausted with slowly emerging forms that will not deny their past. I may scrape them or build them prouder and more complete. It may take weeks or months to finish. I must ponder over them, awaken them, and be awakened . . . the past giving depth to the present.

San Remos took a long time to emerge. I was after a floating and moving form, inseparable from the total image. Inspired by Rembrandt, the master of dramatic light, I wanted this floating form to give light, and dying, lose itself in eternity. When it was finished, it reminded me of the warm glow in a dingy bar, or the street lamp outside one, and so I name it *San Remos*, after a little bar.

critic's comments

Ordinarily a cause is considered in the temporal succession of events to precede the effect. And although this distinction of cause and effect may be one to simply facilitate the analytical functioning of the mind, having no basis in the real world, we frequently experience a reversal of the process. Events and experiences which are yet to transpire become a cause in the future, bringing about effects in action and thought in the present.

Just as this is true of our everyday life, it is also true in the life of the painter, but with this difference: the painter frequently may be troubled by rather vague feelings, feelings which may not be attached to some dramatic situation, but rather to some relationship of color, texture and line. Where this relationship existed may well have been forgotten, and even what the relationships were attached to, whether it was form or light.

In this painting, *San Remos*, there is an image, a configuration of red that emerges from the background, which defies immediate intellectual identification, looming like a monolith in a murky sea of atmosphere. Most of the movements opposing this monolith arise from the diagonal strokes at the base of the painting, directing the eye from left to right. With further study a figure is discernible, center left, whose motion is undeniable, that adds to the mystery of the sensuous response.

san remos by Karla Moss. Top award in Exhibition of the Richmond Art Center, Richmond, California.

statements by the judges

The painting, *San Remos*, by Karla Moss, is the work of an artist who is seriously concerned with the growth and development of the painting: in the powerful juxtaposition of opposites, in the creation of images which set up deep psychological reverberations in the viewer, and in using the methods of the Surrealist (but with a more basic and immediate use of form).

BOYD ALLEN
Berkeley, California

Karla Moss's painting seems to exemplify the general attitude of the young painter of the San Francisco Bay Area . . . it is a concern for the essence of form, a distilate of thought and reaction to nature and its various aspects. Add to this a penetrating insight for the bold and uncluttered . . . that which seeks the central core, and you have the painting, *San Remos*.

The pale pastiche of pink patios and sunsets has been replaced by a vivid and biting charge. This is the new realism.

CLAYTON PINKERTON
Portola Valley, California

jon
naberezny

Mr. Naberezny is now Chairman of the Fine Arts Department of The Youngstown University, Youngstown, Ohio.

statement by the artist

Unfortunately, most observers rarely become aware of the sensitivity involved in the creation of a work of art. This is only natural, since what they see or hear is a completed and organized form, and they must approach it with respect to this completion. They should analyze it as a composed unit for its strength in design, for its unification of related shapes with variation of interest, and for the emotional content of its hues.

They should try to realize that a work of art is a total composition or form which is uniquely organized, and that it becomes a visual sensation of created images of the artist's experiences.

Since my paintings are what I feel rather than only what I see, I find beauty and significance in abstract form.

Crucifixion is a poetic arrangement of forms and colors that give me the feeling and the emotional content of a particular event relative to the Crucifixion. The reds and oranges used in the cruciform pattern express the totality of the emotions involved, while the yellows, ochres, and whites vivify the glorification given to the Crucifixion.

An artist should never have to evaluate his own work, since he is unable to put into verbal form (unless he is a poet) the feeling and the intimacy involved in his own creation.

critic's comments

One of the most pernicious forms of criticism rampant today bases its judgment not on the intentions of the painter visible in the picture, but on the title which to their minds carries with it a categorical *ought* as to what the picture should look like. This "ought" can account for much misunderstanding of the painter, and, what is worse, posthumous appreciation. Thus the past, out of which this "ought" proceeds, cuts the contemporary out of the active present to the impoverishment of public and painter alike.

This painting of the "Crucifixion" obviously has no intention of creating a dramatic spectacle (which alas is more often a still from a tableau than a painting) for didactic or emotional purposes to give the spectator a sense of "being there". Rather, this is an intellectual painting, which attempts to present the Idea.

One reason that the subject of the Crucifixion appears rather late in Christian iconography is the theological problems involved. In presenting the Crucifixion as the Logos, the figure stands free, frontal and without pain. It is not until the Son of Man becomes the victim on the cross that suffering is introduced as an emotive factor.

By returning to one of the earliest conceptions of the Crucifixion, this painting avoids some of the theological questions in dealing with the subject as a timeless condition. Timeless because the elements whereby we fix time in painting are played down as far as possible, i.e., movement and space, and this the painting has in common with the Byzantine tradition.

Further in common is the basic mistrust of the senses as a means of arriving at reality. This mistrust of the human sensory apparatus ultimately culminated in Justinian's late endorsement of the Monophysitic heresy which denied the humanity of Christ.

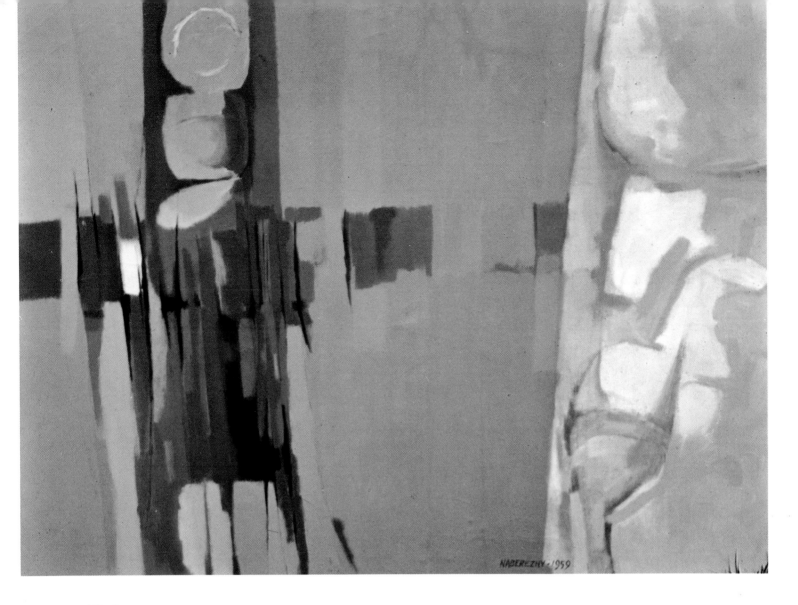

crucifixion by Jon Naberezny. Top award in *Fall Show, Canton Art Institute, Canton, Ohio.*

statement by the judge

More than any other work in the Canton Art Institute Fall Show, *Crucifixion,* by Jon Naberezny, reflected a real and successful concern for painting . . . as painting. While essentially a two-dimensional statement, it evokes at the same time a subtly ambiguous space. However, avoiding the literal as he does, Mr. Naberezny has nonetheless captured a hint of the dramatic import of the subject matter that the title suggests.

The organization is deceptively simple: tensions of thoughtfully placed, near-vertical axes that divide the composition into distinct stripe-like areas, countered by an intermittent horizontal axis that provides a strong integrative force. Free and active subdivisions of the major areas give a surface embroidery that is needed to enliven the picture,

and a subtle reiteration of simple shapes from part to part further insures unity in the strongly differentiated components.

Mr. Naberezny's handling of color is very able, both from a technical and an aesthetic standpoint. The comparatively simple harmonies, ranging from intense red to warm gray, maintain a liveliness that pervades the entire surface, without awkward pockets that could detract from the richness of the whole.

This is a picture that has formal rightness, without fanfare, and a quiet, unassuming authority, but at the same time a compelling vitality which made it clearly deserving of the prize it was given.

PAUL B. ARNOLD, Judge
Oberlin College
Oberlin, Ohio

leroy
neiman

Mr. Neiman is presently a
member of the faculty of
the Art Institute,
Chicago, Illinois.

statement by the artist

What is apparent to the senses when one comes upon a scene for the first time is far different from that experienced upon familiarity. Having allowed myself total impact of new surroundings, the effect remains while things become clear, describable and different upon adjustment. The appearance of shapes and objects immediately or quickly experienced compared with those realized and studied is extraordinary. Here lies the prime objective of my work . . . this phenomenon of change.

The spectator meeting a painting of mine must deal with the same circumstance of change. Areas are broken up at close range and fit together only at a distance. Ready recognition of key elements is difficult because of a certain lack of clearness. Important elements are frequently repressed and the unimportant often stressed in order to bring out the main elements in a hidden way. The idea is not to be "unclear" but to make clarity look like an accident. An averted or shadowed face may contain a chief expression.

I seek to make the task of the spectator increasingly difficult. I set traps for him. Modeling takes place where emphasis does not lie; accents are subordinated; foreground and background merge up close, and then expand with distance. As one advances on a painting it becomes more abstract, more fluid, and as one moves away it falls into focus and is realistic. It is baroque. By venturing into and penetrating the painting, the spectator discovers for himself new substances and has a prolonged contact. At no two distances will the painting be the same.

These plastic qualities of my painting coincide with the realities of contemporary society and its rapidly moving, shifting and ever-changing panorama. Today's man accepts many casual observations, and oftentimes the real truths escape him if he does not take the time to look beneath the surface.

I always sketch from life on location and develop paintings from these drawings later in my studio. *Orchestra* is the result of a visit made to Chicago's CBS Television Studio. From a catwalk above the sound stage I did some drawings of a full dance orchestra then on the show, "In Town Tonight". The rhythmic movement of the musicians, the maze of color plus the loud, brassy sounds excited me. The drawings worked, and I set to work on the painting immediately that night.

Always in my painting, the will prevails for the perfection of explicit representation and a communication with the viewer.

critic's comments

The mutual reactions of painting and music have been long and fruitful, from Egyptian tomb paintings to Van Eyck; from Caravaggio to Picasso. In most instances where the works have survived, there has been a hearty respect for the limitations of both the arts.

Color hearing, however, is a psychological condition which both Rimbaud and Kandinsky attempted to postulate and utilize: Rimbaud, attempting to assign warmth and coolness of color to the sound of a vowel, and Kandinsky, drawing such analogies as the color red with the sound of a trumpet.

orchestra by LeRoy Neiman. Top award in Exhibition North Mississippi Valley Artists, Illinois State Museum, Springfield, Illinois.

For the most part, however, painters have been content to try to translate their musical excitement into good composition; and musical composers may base their analogies on the mood of a painting, realizing that the climax they reach in time is of a different order and intensity than the painting.

The excitement in the painting, *Orchestra*, is primarily color excitement, an interpenetrating red to orange area with a midnight blue to cerulean, the brass section to the right almost completely swallowed in red, while the figure at the drums and cymbals is deep in the blue light. The figures in the orchestra are well-drawn, but since the same liberty that was exercised in the color is not shown in the gestures of the orchestra, it must be assumed that the excitement of the painter, and not the players is the chief communication.

statement by juror

The oil painting, *Orchestra*, by LeRoy Neiman was chosen for its apt illustration of its chosen title, for its sharp rich contrasts in color which expressed sound and movement, and for its excellent paint quality.

FRANCES RIDGELY
for the foreman of the Jury

jurors

Anonymous, Foreman of the Jury; Thomas Devel, Illinois State Museum; Frances Ridgely, Illinois State Museum.

willis
nelson

Mr. Nelson is currently an instructor of painting, sculpture and prints at the Wisconsin State College and Instructor of Technology, Platteville, Wisconsin. He is listed in Who's Who in American Art.

statement by the artist

The major problem of today's artist is to create a timely reality, to manifest the "new poetry" that scientific discovery has added to the visual and non-visual worlds. Whether he manipulates form from an existing reality and uses it metaphorically or attempts a disassociation from illusion of forms that do exist is not the important problem. To present his way of feeling and thinking and to confirm his individuality in each new work within the realm of the atmosphere of his time is to me the important problem.

What influences affect the artist's work do not matter as long as the work expresses the "language of the day." I have been influenced by the poetic finesse and atmospheric subtleties of Chinese landscape painting. A unity of Oriental poetic depth with a more vigorous and dynamic Western impact. Nature is the theme . . . to be aware of the movement of prairie grass set in motion by a gentle breeze or gale-like forces. The forms I seek are those that will best express the life cycle and moods of nature, life, growth, death, decay, and multivaried forms that nature provides. I do not want to paint the tree's exterior, its bark, or leaves. This is "ready made" beauty, too obvious and even "trite" with its ever-abundant presence. I would rather turn over a rotting log to see where the elements have been at work unseen, such as the beauty of fungus growing over vermiculated and discolored wood.

Point of Separation was painted with the sensation of the idea being as important as the pictorial effects by which the idea was elaborated. They were merged to create an organic statement about life without becoming too literal. A piece of nature seen both specific and generalized. Microscopic nature, blown up to visual apprehension. A process of nature, a division on a non-visual level. It could be a division by decay. The separation of ideas or a bit of nature split asunder by explosive powers. The destruction that the naked eye misses when the Bomb goes off.

statement by judge

It is comparatively simple to explicate the reasons why I gave *Point of Separation* first prize in the Wisconsin 25th Annual Art Salon. It caught my attention and had the power to retain it in spite of the many good works which surrounded it.

To explain what it was that made it stand out demands that we examine its structure and attempt to translate its nonverbal stimulations into ideas which words can express. What we notice, of course, is the sensitivity which permits the artist to suggest what appears to be a whole spectrum of colors by the subtle manipulation of an earth-like brown. It is diffused throughout the canvas and becomes, by turns, darker then lighter, suggesting now a solid, then suddenly becoming an infinite space. It is torn asunder and contained by a mist of white. It is made cool by a glow of orange, and is warmed by tiny blue-charged fields.

Unexplainably, we are made to feel that the artist has immobilized an awesome thought. The colors alternately seem to congeal into recognizable forms, and these shapes in turn appear to have been

point of separation by Willis Nelson. Top award in Wisconsin Salon of Art, University of Wisconsin, Madison, Wisconsin.

caught in the midst of explosion. Is it the essence of autumn that the artist has distilled for us? . . . dried up, splitting, broadcasting next season's life? We have here nature and her forces in transition, caught in the act of dying and becoming: the seed pod bursting, the cell in fission, an explosive force sending particles in all directions.

All these ideas are suggested within the static form of square canvas. But look again. Even the shape of the canvas reflects the theme. The width is slightly longer than the height, subtly reinforcing the feeling of expansion. Each element within the frame is so placed that the theme is never lost. We see, and are made to feel, contained dispersion at every point in a myriad different ways. In short, the

artist reveals himself to have a full and sensitive control of his medium, his craft, his expression.

The painting strikes me as a complete and masterful visual statement, sufficient unto itself. It arouses that indescribable pleasure expected of art, which simultaneously calms and excites.

ORAZIO FUMAGALLI, Judge
Curator, Tweed Gallery
University of Minnesota, Duluth

judges

Byron Burford, University of Iowa; Ray H. French, DePauw University; Orazio Fumagalli, University of Minnesota.

In 1957, Mr. Pachner began teaching at the Tampa Art Institute and established the William Pachner School of Art, Clearwater, Florida. He is listed in Who's Who in American Art.

statement by the artist

In periods past the artist painted for the glory of God. His work was his declaration of faith, his prayer, his confession. We may be embarrassed to use such terminology in our age, but has the nature of the artist's occupation changed fundamentally? Does it really matter what we call it? I feel that by whatever term it goes, the artist at work now or at any time in our history is functioning in much the same way.

We are the people of transition; we are witnessing a complete remaking of the world. Ties and substances seem to be disintegrating. The true artist, perhaps the most truly conscious member of his society, by projecting his tensions and anxieties, projects often what the society is experiencing as a whole. His hand is the hand of a seismograph. The essence of the creative attitude remains unaltered . . . a responsive merging of the individual with immediate everyday experience.

critic's comments

Like the prologue in an Elizabethan drama, or the chorus in a Greek play, the donor on the left side of the *Villa Nueve Pieta* introduces the spectator to the tragic group, Christ and his Mother, Saints Magdalene and John. In the "Variation" the donor is missing, for there is no need of an intermediary. As in *King Lear*, when the action moves to its terrible climax, the "fool" disappears, for any mirth would become grotesque. The only alleviation possible is a technical one, the relief of prose. The only relief in the non-temporal "Variation" is to watch the images swell into being and then ebb into another shape.

The corpse of Christ is the most solidly discernible figure, with its rigid white torso swelling into an arc of whiteness that turns at the thigh into the stringy anatomy of a flayed leg as it moves downward toward the earth. The right arm is lost in darkness and is only resumed as a forearm and clenched fist. And what was once a triangle of the Virgin's cloak now rises menacingly alone like another arm to crucify the Dead Figure again. Above this triangle a spectral head emerges that seems to be desperately pointing to a fish being held aloft in the right hand of St. John. But is this St. John who moves so transparently? Could it be the boy with the loaves and fishes who provided the food for a miracle? If this is not St. John, then what is this monstrous blackness supporting the head of the corpse that rises through the transparent boy like some ancient Bull with a succession of masks from the fiends of hell?

And then . . . there are no haloes . . . and we are not looking at one pieta only; we are looking down past the written ages of man, past the literal memory to the tannist, to the surrogate to the ritual slaughter, for this is no weeping Magdalene over the body, but a shaman with a scythe, behind whose head is the incessant repetition of horns. Below the shaman is a figure reminiscent from Rembrandt's *Descent from the Cross* (1632). I have no doubt that this is an inspired painting.

variation on the avignon pieta no. 2 by William Pachner. Top award in Midyear Show, The Butler Institute of American Art, Youngstown, Ohio.

statement by judge

William Pachner's *Variation on the Avignon Pieta No. 2* was awarded as a most arresting piece of abstract imagery, powerfully colored and constructed. This approach to a tender subject is moving and sensitive. It is, in effect, as representational as a non-objective painting can become! This pieta is seemingly a different and difficult approach, yet successful in the idea it conveys, as well as the thought it stimulates.

Of the 1,500 oils examined by the Jury, Pachner's work was considered outstanding in its category.

Jos. G. Butler

judges

Joseph T. Fraser, Jr., Pennsylvania Academy of Fine Art, Philadelphia, Pennsylvania; Everett Spruce, University of Texas, Austin, Texas. Jos. G. Butler, Foreman of the Jury. The Butler Institute of American Art, Youngstown, Ohio.

guy palazzola

Mr. Palazzola is now Assistant Professor of Art at the University of Michigan, Ann Arbor, Michigan.

statement by the artist

I don't like to think of myself as a particular type of painter. I would rather try to search out what I like to do in paint without attachment to so-called "main streams" in today's art.

Somewhere in the quiet reflections of a person must lie truth and integrity. This is what I hope to find . . . and in so proceeding take the risk of becoming banal or non-contemporary.

To me, a painting is at once a composition and a performance. The painter is at once the author and the virtuoso, and his standard can only be excellence.

Art, simple, direct, and unadorned, can be superlative, but the major work holds within it complexities bound into a synthesis that to me is excellence. Most of what we artists do today seems to me to be epigrammatic and anecdotal. We cite what is incidental and exotic. Art derived from a selection here and there of isolated glimpses, for me cannot be major. It is only so when it is a seasoned distillation of many possibilities.

My painting, *Sponge of Vinegar*, is one of the moments in my career where I have attempted to record the beauty and charm of an object. The fascination derived from the actual properties of the sponge led to painting it. Beyond that I saw a symbolization of the Crucifixion. I felt that these qualities presented a technical and aesthetic challenge that could only be resolved through the most assiduous realism. The accomplishment of this provided me keen satisfaction and enjoyment.

critic's comments

We are all familiar with the various uses of the sponge . . . around the house, in the garage, in the sick room, in the gym. But these uses are not the meaning of the sponge, for it can become an ascription of a human parasite, a token of defeat, or the condition of bread that has been leavened just before kneading. Finally, it is a symbol of the Passion, where on a reed it carried vinegar to Christ dying on the cross. The latter is what this painting conveys.

Magic Realism, which is the school of painting this picture would fall under, attempts to render the image more intensely real by concentrating on sharp focus, textural differentiations, and a familiar aspect of the objects. The space appears to be the kind of space we move in. And the objects offer the implied tactual responses we are accustomed to experiencing. But if this is true, why do we not pass by the painting as we probably would pass by a sponge carelessly left in a crockery bowl?

By comparison, the skill of Magic Realism becomes unpretentious, with no impediment to the act of identification and recognition. And once this is accomplished, the spectator is in a position to go beyond his own past experience with the objects, and by subtraction find what the painter is revealing. There is a reddish taint to the color of vinegar which clinches his apprehension that this is not the usual sponge. He may go further and draw an analogy between the leaven, the metaphor for evil, and the sponge as the symbol of defeat.

One thing is certain: he will never again experience the sponge as just a sponge.

sponge of vinegar by Guy Palazzola. Top award in West Michigan Art Exhibition, Grand Rapids Art Gallery, Grand Rapids, Michigan.

statement by critic

The striking subject matter . . . in addition to the technique . . . probably snared the judges' attention and favor here.

judges

Edward Dwight, Milwaukee Art Center, Milwaukee, Wisconsin; Joseph Cox, School of the Art Institute, Chicago, Illinois.

ambrose patterson

For twenty-eight years, Mr. Patterson taught at the School of Art, University of Washington, retiring as Professor Emeritus in Painting in 1947. At 83, he is indulging to the fullest in his life-long dream of "doing nothing but painting." He is listed in Who's Who in American Art.

statement by the artist

The oil painting, *Interior*, the result of an instinctive impulse, was developed imaginatively with a free elimination of detail, and the stress of certain others, but above all the avoidance of too literal a statement.

I wished, however, in spite of the liberties I have taken (technically) for *Interior* to express a certain feeling I had of the subject, and I therefore regard it as a true representation of my living room.

critic's comments

In the critical remarks on the painting, *San Remos*, there is briefly noted the peculiar time-transcendence of cause and effect in the conception of a painting, that a picture literally progresses in time to go forth to meet its origin in the future. Now a similar thing occurs in the relationship between paintings of the past and of the present. To say that the Vermeer we see today is not the Vermeer seen in the nineteenth century may sound absurd. To be sure, if there is such a thing as a pure retinal image, perhaps this remains the same, even making allowances for the changes in color brought about by time and chemistry; but, can we see Vermeer independently of Mondrian? Has not Mondrian actually changed Vermeer? Can we see Cezanne independently of the Cubists? Thus it is that the past not only has the power to effect a change in the present, but that the present is continually altering the past. Vision operates within vision, expanding, interpreting and interpenetrating . . . truly a world in and out of time.

For the sake of narrative clarity, Giotto frequently removed the sides of houses to reveal an interior event, necessary to the dramatic continuity of the action. Later in the Renaissance, the interior gains in importance plastically for the space it affords the forms, and psychologically as an index reflecting the mood of the composition. A marked change occurs in the interiors as painted by the Dutch in the seventeenth century. In the painting of church interiors, Pieter Saenredam reduces the figures in his compositions to one of the most abstract of function.

In the present painting, *Interior*, there is a similarity of color harmony to Saenredam in the domination of the cool tones. So well-chosen is the relationship of warm to cool that the feeling of morning light is quite precise. The composition converges on a vertical axis just left of center, with a secondary movement toward the blue rectangle at the far left. Relieving the severity of the right angles and near right angles that by color contrasts continue to return the eye to the surface of the painting, is the arabesque of curvilinear shapes that describe the chair, piano, and flower arrangements. The intriguing quality of these curves is their ability to become descriptive and then return to their abstract state.

interior by Ambrose Patterson. Top award in Seattle Art Museum, Seattle, Washington.

statement by judge

At the 1959 Exhibition, I was particularly engaged by the fine painting, *An Interior*, by Ambrose Patterson.

The painting expresses the gentler natural aspects of the coastal Pacific Northwest. The filtered light of Seattle summer morning is quite eloquently conveyed through the use of gray tones heightening to white; and warming color accents define the "immobiles" of the composition, i.e., grand piano, bookshelves, etc., . . . one of which, an elegantly curving long, low rocking chaise, seems still to rock, and commands singularly the idea of human presence although no human form is employed in the composition except through the use of a whitish sculptured torso form.

In it one feels, too, a distinct feeling of flowering . . . this region's profuse flowering reflected inside a room. This is effected through a series of drawing definitions and accents with warm colors distributed artfully throughout the essentially neutral picture space.

The painting is, I feel, firmly founded in European and American painting traditions. It appears to be seen through the eye, and constructed through the intellect of a painter conversant with past and current directions; and finally, although not a radical departure from the treatment of such a subject, let us say, by Matisse, it is originally conceived and personally carried out . . . and has something of a "new" contemporaneousness in its human suggestion and subject. It seems, indeed, to be the work of a highly skilled, long-informed craftsman.

LEON APPLEBAUM

judges

Max W. Sullivan, Portland Art Museum, Portland, Oregon; Wendell P. Brazeua, University of Washington; Robert Feasley, Washington State University; James Lee Hansen, Vancouver, Washington; Leon Applebaum.

donna
perkins

Miss Perkins is now living
in Freeport, Illinois.

statement by the artist

I experiment continually, and have no set technique or fixed palette. I paint on masonite, and each painting begins with the sketch or sketches and then evolves its own technique. It may call for oil or casein, or both; and it may require the use of brushes or palette knives or even the palm of the hand. I would rather paint a dangerous, insecure picture than one that is safe. When a painter becomes frightened and careful, all feeling disappears from the canvas.

I find textures extremely exciting, and find that paint quality, texture, and design mean more to me than subject matter.

When I finish a painting, I'm exhilarated and delighted; but this delight soon fades. Within a short time, I lose this feeling and start to look for mistakes. Soon the painting becomes merely an alluring surface . . . an exciting basis for a new painting.

South Side is painted over *The Quiet Time* which was accepted and hung in *ART: USA: 58.* I have a number of exhibition pictures that have disappeared under new paintings.

In painting over other earlier paintings, I have found my own personal technique . . . although I use other techniques beside this. When I paint over another picture and then scrape down to exciting color below, the surface becomes alive. The top colors are either more subtle or more brilliant, and the picture begins to have a life of its own. The paint surface and the texture are very important to what I want to say in paint. My one personal aim is to improve and to grow . . . to add something vital to this wonderful world we live in.

critic's comments

There is an uncanny quiet about this painting, *South Side*, with its muted colors and right angular emphases, that build up suddenly and almost unexpectedly into a sense of dread . . . similar, we expect, to the sense of dread and awe felt by those investigators who first climbed aboard the "Marie Celeste" in mid-ocean, to find a ship adrift without crew or passengers, and with no sign of violence or eminent danger, for the afternoon meal was prepared and still warm. What happened? No one knows. All they heard was the sigh of the wind in the rigging and the ghostly slap of the water against the hull. On looking again at *South Side*, one wonders if the wind increases or alleviates the sense of desolation, for there is no sign of movement here.

Compositionally, what constitutes this silence made visible affords a very interesting problem. The "stop" gate in the immediate foreground offers the first clue, for the lines at either end form brief diagonals in reverse perspective, which, instead of converging on the painting, converge on the spectator. This convergence tends to make the spectator overlook the slight hints of diagonal ruts leading across the tracks and into a point just left of the dominant telephone pole. Further, these diagonals are stopped by three of the darkest color contrasts in the form of the two boxcars and a coal car, and the three sets of two cross-arms on the poles.

These cross-arms are strategically placed. Their repetition arrests the eye long enough to focus on a near-blue and a near-violet area.

It then is compelled to move to the largest near-complementary area of yellow to the right. Because the eye is carrying a yellow after-image from its resting point of the telephone poles, it sees the yellow as being more intense than it actually is. The red cells of the eye are then alerted to the linear movement and contrast immediately above and to the left of the yellow car, and begin to move counter clockwise

back into the picture to begin the exploration again.

Each strong, linear movement is counteracted either by a color or by a right angle. This is so deftly accomplished that the eye of the spectator soon settles to rest in the central gray-white texture, to enjoy an unearthly quiet, as though he were a new Adam.

south side by Donna Perkins. *Top award winner in Rockford and Vicinity Show, Burpee Art Gallery, Rockford, Illinois.*

statement by judge

Her work is of a professional status. It is fresh, vital, and creative. She deserves to be numbered among the vital artists of today.

SISTER M. THOMASITA, O.S.F.,
Art Dept., Cardinal Stritch College, Milwaukee, Wisconsin

the judges

Richard A. Florsheim, Contemporary Art Workshop, Chicago, Illinois; Sister Mary Thomasita, Cardinal Stritch College; Alfred Sessler, University of Wisconsin.

walter plate

Mr. Plate lives in Woodstock, New York with his wife, Gladys Brodsky . . . also a painter . . . and their two sons.

statement by the artist

I personally believe that only a poet with as inventive a mind for words as the artist has for color and composition can say a truth about today's painting. There has been a lot of talking done on the subject of abstraction in art, but, so far, I feel that only the paintings themselves have been eloquent.

critic's comments

From the red geranium planted in a discarded lard can to the philodendron in the drawing room; from the row of zinnias in the garden patch to the clipped boxwoods of the formal gardens, is evidence enough that man's love of plants goes beyond the strictly utilitarian. If one started from the present to explore this love, either subjectively or in literature and painting, how long would it be before the searching mind would touch some fragment of memory leading to that delicate tracery of feeling inherited from the past of Greece? A tracery that by an act of poetic intuition links man and plant together in the common bond of mortality. The nymphs of the sea, mountains, rivers, brooks and grottoes were all considered to be immortal, but the Dryads came into being with the tree and expired with it. Is not a further kinship with the plant world evidenced today in the desire to bring nature into the house? Is it that man's self-conscious eminence in nature has made him lonely?

Man seeks to assuage his loneliness in many ways: some rush in to the frantic world of change where success is measured in the more of today against the balance of yesterday; or they quietly turn to the eternal world where past, present and future lose their identity and are gathered together in one great "now".

If plants measure time in terms of seasonal change, then how is time measured in a hot house? Is not succession then one of growth and the season the eternal "now" of summer? Just as when we step into a "hot house" we step into a world that is no longer measured by our minutes and seconds of clock time: so it is when we contemplate the painting, *Hot House*. Because we correlate duration as the fourth dimension of the three dimensions of space, the absence of an implied three-dimensional space appears to arrest the passage of time. The spectator has no set point of observation but exists equally at all points. There are allusions in the painting to pots and plants, but in the hot compressed space their scale is as difficult to discern as though we were outside the building and seeing the objects through a steam-laden piece of glass. This is important to the success of the painting, for particularity at this point would be at variance to the very specific sensory experience which the painter wishes to convey. Is it by nature or by choice that we are on the outside looking in?

hot house by Walter Plate. Top award in The 26th Biennial Exhibition of Contemporary American Painting, The Corcoran Gallery of Art.

statement by judge

Perhaps the most striking quality of the painting, *Hot House*, by Walter Plate, is the obvious control demonstrated by the artist throughout the painting in spite of its imposing size (72″x96″) and the free handling of the medium.

The immediate appeal of bold contrast and spontaneous brushwork puts the artist, for the moment at least, in the camp of the abstract expressionist. Yet, the strength of the work is by no means due to happy accidents but to the realization of carefully thought-out composition and a distribution of color areas reminiscent of the work of the cubists.

HERMAN WARNER WILLIAMS, JR.,
Director, The Corcoran Gallery of Art

judges

Charles Edward Buckley, Currier Gallery of Art, Manchester, New Hampshire; Allen Stuart Weller, University of Illinois; Herman Warner Williams, Jr., Director, The Corcoran Gallery of Art.

89

marlyn prior

Mrs. Prior is now working toward an M.A. degree at Long Beach State College. She lives in Rolling Hills Estates, California.

statement by the artist

This painting was begun the summer of 1958 and painted in several stages throughout 1959. Several concepts were of concern to me in creating this work. I was interested in composing a painting with the major emphasis near the top, to be balanced by a large expanding area flowing to the lower edge of the composition. I selected pieces of gnarled wood, dried desert plants, rocks, and a bone, which I placed on newspapers on the floor. Thus my angle of observation of the still-life arrangement was from above, looking down. The major areas of the painting were freely sketched in with brush and thin paint with no preparatory sketches. Color areas were built up gradually, and as the work progressed, I sensed the need for stronger opposing forms to balance the objects at the top. I worked with a limited palette, tending towards a predominance of orange and browns. The painting was completed when I felt all the parts of the composition appeared united and the painting seemed to emerge as a whole. I felt that *Desert Forms* was a step towards a more dynamic organization, fluidity, and forcefulness in my painting.

An interest in landscape forms has motivated my painting in the last few years. My work tends to follow a pattern . . . to examine the detail of rocks and roots, then widen to the panoramic view, and concentrate again on the smaller elements of landscape forms. For me each painting must have a unity of idea, technique, and emotion. I conceive of an idea, and consider it for a long time before it emerges in a painting. As in *Desert Forms*, the subject matter is interpreted here to include my personal feeling for the tangled forms found on the desert.

critic's comments

Haunted by the interminable possibility that he may be the accidental product of the blind machinations of the unconscious Ananke, Goddess of Chance, set adrift in limitless ocean of space, with no sentient Being higher than his own to listen as he sings his bright dreams or prays his brave thoughts, Man fears that the finale to his brief symphony, instead of being the jubilant chorus of glad hosannas, will be the simple, measured, though unheard by himself, tolling of the bell. To the religious the act of Faith and the act of knowledge are, indeed, synonymous, for along the way the intellectual distinctions fade and crumble in the contemplation of the holy.

But to the painter, the act of painting is an act of faith . . . faith not only that there is a material world which sponsors his sensations, but faith that the world he values, whether it receives cosmic support or not, can become, *through* his act, tangent to the material world, even if this tangency is as brief as his action. Brief though it be, the life of the world has reflected back the life of the spirit, and preserved in the brilliance of the painting as an act of knowledge.

Here two great rhythms are harnessed . . . one, the rhythm of weathering and erosion, and two, the violent insurgence of life toward survival. There is always the great temptation to think that one rhythm exists for the sustenance of the other, that the great cracking, splintering rocks exist for the plants. Why is it that we are so averse to thinking that this rock was once the dust of a dead plant?

desert forms by (Mrs.) Marlyn Prior. Top award in Long Beach Juried Exhibition, Long Beach Museum of Art, Long Beach, California.

statement by critic

This rather spectacular combination of contrasting elements was undoubtedly recognized because of its rhythm and construction.

jurors

Lorser Feitelson, Los Angeles, California; Dr. F. M. Hinkhouse, Phoenix Fine Arts Association, Phoenix, Arizona; Henry Seldis, Los Angeles, California.

robert d. ray

Mr. Ray is now living in Taos, New Mexico. He is listed in Who's Who in American Art.

statement by the artist

The mountains surrounding Taos, New Mexico, are called the Sangre de Cristo Range . . . a particularly apt name for two reasons. During certain times of the year the reflection of the setting sun turns the earth and rocks of these mountains a blood red. Located in this particular area is also a group of Spanish-Americans known as Los Hermanos Penitentes. This is a local religious order, Roman Catholic, and indirectly derived from the Third Order of Saint Francis. It is a flagellant group which used to literally re-enact the Passion of Christ during the Lenten season. The practices became so brutal that they were banned by the church. However, a Papal decree in 1947 accepted them, provided that a less severe form be followed.

Today, a very moving ceremony may be observed on Good Friday. A symbolic re-enactment of the Crucifixion is performed, using a severely beautiful, carved, painted Christ which is jointed so that it may be removed from the cross. The ceremony is read in Spanish from an old copy book with a hand-written text. Music is solemnly chanted accompanied by fiddle and home-made flute.

But the severe harshness of this particular area is still wedded to the flagellant penitente, and it is this perfect mating of a culture to its environment that I wanted to express in this painting.

critic's comments

Most of us at one time or the other have wanted to see the world as it appeared when it was young. There is that desire, even if only in the imagination, to be a lonely Adam on some promontory and experience the world in all its freshness, as though another presence would taint the objectivity of the vision, which we may feel is so often shattered today by the wail of a siren or the insistent honking of a horn. If we look to science for a reconstruction of this possible Adamic experience, we may put the book down with our factual curiosity satisfied, but with our senses searching for a resting place like a mountain climber's foot feeling for the solidity of rock over the ledge. What we are searching for are facts that carry the force of emotional conviction. In experiencing a painting the emotional conviction is validated by how well the senses other than sight corroborate the image. Touch is frequently called on to verify the fallible eye.

No one can look at this painting, *Sangre de Cristo Range*, and not feel the sense of touch reinforcing the sense of visual space. The space in this painting is achieved by the graduation of the widths of the line and the degrees of roughness of the texture. The eye accepts this convention of space by the implication of linear direction or value and textural contrasts, by the analogy of its experience with nature. With these means the painter has produced an image of mountains in a light and space peculiar to the western United States, a space wherein there is no vegetation to mitigate the thrust of the rough mountains toward the sky. So arid and forbidding is this prospect that man feels his body as the only living bond between sky and earth. Perhaps it is this aridity which tells him of a loneliness on earth in a world not made for man. But was it not after the grandiose spectacles of nature that the "still, small voice" sounded to heal the breach between the temporal and the eternal?

sangre de cristo range by Robert D. Ray. Top award in Circle Invitational Exhibition, Roswell, New Mexico.

statement by judge

Ray presents an interesting case in current American painting, in that he generally retains a reference to subject matter (in his case the Southwest), although he is by no means a representational painter. Offhand, I would say his major asset is in his tactile quality, and the subtle aspect of his color. These two aspects are combined together to produce a really "classic" quality in all of his paintings which I have experienced.

> DAVID GEBHARD, Director
> Roswell Museum and Art Center
> Roswell, New Mexico

judges

Acquisitions Committee, Roswell Museum: Irving Baranchick, Chairman; Mrs. Donald B. Anderson; Sim B. Christy; Mrs. Don Gillespie, Jr.; Mrs. E. W. Lander; Bill Wiggins; Mrs. Peter Hurd.

david schnabel

Mr. Schnabel *now lives in*
Altadena, California.

statement by the artist

In my painting, it is my hope to wed the freedoms of the present
with the disciplines of the past. It is not inconsistent to learn from
Kline and DeKooning while making a serious study of the underpaint-
ing and over-glazing of Titian and Tintoretto. Thus, I've learned a
lot from the "action" painters even though feeling little kinship with
their point of view. I can appreciate the value of following sponta-
neously, absolutely, instantaneously the impulse of arm, fingers, brush,
seemingly guided by someone else; yet at the same time I'm impelled
to believe that my greatest strength lies in restraint and my greatest
power in planning. I've been trying to use these seemingly divergent
elements to weave a strong fabric, hoping to achieve a spontaneous
freedom within the framework of a planned painting.

The figure has been the motivating force in most of my work, and
while keenly aware of the dominant non-figurative direction of much
contemporary painting and appreciative of some of it, I've always been
impelled to paint man, and have rarely been drawn to anything that
did not concern him and his life. This is so, even with the cold impersonality of the armored man, the medieval *Guardsman;* a creature with
a formidable facade of metal and rich embellishment; a form curiously
impersonal, bedecked to destroy in an impersonal way, without specific anger or knowledge of his foe. He is like a bejeweled peacock;
strangely beautiful, costumed for death, yet we see here in this prelude
to battle only the glint of armor with no hint as to the nature of the
man within.

critic's comments

The strength of this painting is twofold: the daring with which
the painter has employed an image that has a long and rich history,
but which also has the danger of appearing as an anachronism . . .
and the taking of this potentially anachronistic image and translating
it into a contemporary painterly idiom and maintaining the integrity
of this synthesis. The image we are possibly more familiar with in
literature than in painting, for how much more real to us are the
Arthurean legends than the paintings of the Pre-Raphaelites.

The sense in which the space in this painting is contemporary is
its strict differentiation from architectural or enclosed space, the
space we move in; rather the painting assumes the kind of respect for
the wall as does a mural, wherein space is devised by color contrasts
and value contrasts. Further, the former centrality of humanistic
doctrine is shifted in the direction of the impersonality of geometric
forms. The emotional content is brought about by the solidity we
feel in association with rectangles in contrast to the piercing, penetrating points of the triangles.

What man has added unto himself to reduce his naked vulnerability
in the face of nature stands midway between form and function, a
psychical as well as physical projection, having the magic of morale as
well as the efficiency of action. We move above and below the areas
of our tactual senses, taking pride in our machines that exceed the
grasp of our fingers or the limits of our vision. By them we have
stretched our bodies beyond their natural confines.

guardsman by David Schnabel. Top award in exhibition of All-City Outdoor Art Festival, Los Angeles, California.

statement by judge

The Jury of Awards for the 1959 Annual All-City Outdoor Art Festival unanimously awarded the painting *Guardsman* by David Schnabel the major award for oil painting.

The work by this artist possesses a combination of vitality and sensitivity. The strong semi-abstract quality in the painting is supported with an equally strong sense of underlying structure and the color is striking.

MILLARD SHEETS, Foreman of the Jury

judges

Millard Sheets, Claremont, California; Arthur Millier, Los Angeles, California; Lorser Feitelson, Los Angeles, California.

tony scornavacca

In 1959, Mr. Scornavacca opened the "Scornavacca Gallery," exhibiting his paintings exclusively, in South Miami, Florida. He is presently painting full time.

statement by the artist

My painting is dominated by what is immediately around me, and that which is immediately around me stirs me incessantly to paint: the sea, the sky; the births and the babies; the love and the lovers; the bottles and the boats; the body; the human and the humor; the sand and the sun; the spirit, the sport; the sleep on the sheets; the private prayer; the God; the everything.

This is around me, a natural rhythm of life. I see it, I feel it, I smell it, I hear it, I taste it, I paint it.

critic's comments

Most museum goers who see a Rubens painting for the first time, executed on a panel, and not one that is just a studio product, are astonished and not a little incredulous over its fantastic freshness. Certainly few masters have excelled his vocabulary in the language of paint and what paint is capable of conveying, materially, spatially and texturally.

Blue Seascape incorporates one of the distinctions which Rubens made between opaque, translucent and transparent color . . . that the opaque color describes light and mass, the translucent the transition or middle tones, and the transparent the recessive or shadow areas. This would possibly be irrelevant were it not for the fact that in the hands of this artist the same differentiations of the means bring forth a new and strange world of space that is so evocative of the sea that the medium could be overlooked.

Compositionally, the space is built on a traditional "s" curve. Beginning in white at the upper right third of the panel, the movement continues in white through the first "u" shape of the "s" until it reaches the lower right third where it is picked up by the entering wedge of a violet triangle. This main thematic movement is opposed by three interrupted shapes which begin as blue at the upper center and rush with gathering intensity to the boatlike shape just past center on the left side, where again the movement re-enters the "s" curve.

The horizon line is firmly established at the upper fifth of the painting. But as the eye begins to follow the indication of the composition, a new relationship occurs between the horizon and the directional indication, with the result that the newly established planes do not coincide with the horizon but form new diagonals that place the entire foreground of the painting beneath them. It is as if the water at this point becomes entirely crystalline so that the spectator is below, at, and above the surface. This is further emphasized by the contrasts at the front edge of the white areas, which cause them to float like clouds or scatter like spray. Thus an old method of paint becomes a new geometry of experience.

blue seascape by Tony Scornavacca. *Top award winner in the Southeastern Exhibition, Atlanta Art Association Galleries,* Atlanta, Georgia.

statement by judge

Blue Seascape impressed me most favorably for several reasons. I found it to be a work in which the artist had successfully and subtly blended elements of realism with those of abstract character. The color harmony which he achieved in this painting is remarkably appealing. At a time when many artists seem to be striving self-consciously for effect, this example of Scornavacca's work was outstanding as one marked by great sensitivity and sincerity.   THOMAS C. HOWE, Judge

the judges

Isabel Bishop, Riverdale, New York; Thomas C. Howe, San Francisco, California.

statement by the artist

The painting *Men's Art Club*, in a way, pinpoints the basis of all figurative art, namely drawing. As an artist draws, he will paint likewise. Time has proved this. Virtually all masters, past and present, are identified by their draftsmanship whether it is a pencil note or deeply integrated within the painting framework.

The idea of *Men's Art Club* was generally to register the importance of drawing the human figure, the starting point, and perhaps the finishing point, of all art endeavor. This is a belief I have adhered to in thirty years of painting.

The visual source of *Men's Art Club* was gleaned at a local session of a men's group called "Buckeye Art Club." Grouped around the nude, each is interpreting the subject in his own personal way. Although the painting was done from memory, several good likenesses appear, adding a little something additional to the already human interest.

critic's comments

The composition has been carefully considered and thought out, even though it has all the informality of a life class. The planes of the paint boxes have been so disposed as to lead the eye into the painting. The heads of the painters create an irregular line moving around the model. The five canvases to the right form a triangle, which by its tilt again pulls the eye toward the head of the model. The canvas held by the student in the lower left prevents the two groups from separating, and thus splitting the composition into two pictures, which could easily have happened because of the continuity of the line from the drape above the model's right shoulder, down the arm to the canvas and knee of the seated student. The placing of the warm and cool colors creates lines to oppose the directions already stated.

A visit to any evening art class will substantiate the truth of the gestures of these painters. In fact, so well have they been described that there is a feeling we can recognize individuals in their conscious and unconscious attitudes toward painting . . . and, most important, their attitudes toward the model. The humor is mostly in the contrasts of these attitudes.

The sum total of the gestures of the students adds up to a feeling of uneasiness, as though the group were participating in an activity that is somewhat risque. The battle which Thomas Eakins fought for the nude model is not over, for today there are university art departments where drawing from a nude model is forbidden, and exhibitions where the nude is automatically rejected. The decline of the nude in painting is obvious. Is it that we can only accept some scantily clad female on the cover of a cheap magazine where the motivation is so obviously salacious? It is significant that the most popular sports are the ones where the beauty of the body is most covered.

Thus *Men's Art Club* points up a condition in our society that is not just particular but quite general: the fear, the curiosity, the revulsion, and, all too seldom, the admiration of the human body. We may smile and hang another abstraction on the wall, but the condition remains.

clyde singer

Mr. Singer now lives in Youngstown, Ohio . . . where he works mainly in oil, and averages 60 to 100 paintings a year. He is listed in Who's Who in American Art.

men's art club by Clyde Singer. Top award in Representational Art Annual, Gilcrease Institute of American History and Art, Tulsa, Oklahoma.

statement by the judge

I gave Mr. Clyde Singer's painting *Men's Art Club* top award in the exhibit because it was concerned with all the classic problems of representational art . . . viz . . . subject matter was presented so that it told its "story" clearly, without ambiguity, relations of the representational features were so organized that a creditable design resulted, and the drawing was seriously undertaken. In addition, color was attractive and suitable to the subject. All this is quite rare today among the younger painters.

THOMAS HART BENTON
Kansas City, Missouri

norbert smith

Mr. Smith is now Vice-President and Art Director of Promotional Arts, Inc., Chicago, Illinois.

statement by the artist

The painting, *Little Crucifixion*, is a transcription into visual form of a series of related concepts. I believe that a graphic presentation of material can lead to a clarification of the relationship between concepts, much as a map will clarify relationships between places, even to people who are already familiar with the actual places shown on the map. For this reason, one who has studied a map may have a clearer picture of a given city in his mind than one born and raised in this same city but who has never seen a map of it.

In *Little Crucifixion* I began with certain concepts and explored the relationships between these concepts in graphic terms. The concepts contained in the painting are (1) the Crucifixion; (2) the growth of the various churches following this; (3) simultaneous strength and weakness: Divinity, God portrayed as the Father (the head of an old man, the royal crown, the large hands symbolizing creation) and at the same time humanity (the proportions of the body are those of a child); (4) the voluntary loving background of the action . . . the hand raised in blessing; and (5) the reparation aspect . . . the heart shaped also like the symbolic apple of the Adam and Eve story.

This painting then is didactic: it shows the Crucifixion not as a historical scene, but rather a collection of traditional Christian ideas about the significance of the event. It shows the Crucifixion as a central event in time, beginning with Adam and Eve and continuing through history to the present, where the brilliant colors of the church steeples and domes in the background almost overshadow the central figure. The personal representation of the man Christ is lost, and the two beholders, Mary and John with their immediate grief, almost disappear in the organized structural forms of the churches.

critic's comments

It is scarcely possible to view this painting and not recall the great age of faith that found its expression in twelfth and thirteenth-century stained glass, or even earlier in the many jewel-like tesserae which make up a Byzantine mosaic. The justification here is not merely that oil paint and glazes are capable of assuming the vibrance and luminosity of glass, but that the kind of space created by the transparent and matted glass, crossed by variable cames of lead, can be used more easily for symbolic interpretation than the space of the late Renaissance, which is more in depth than in surface.

There is a Romanesque severity about the crowned head of Christ, delineated in tones of blue which recall the blue hair and beard of the Christ of "Descent into Limbo" at Nea Monis in Chios. The cross itself is only suggested, for a fuller, more obvious statement of the right angles would hinder the movement of light ascending near the head and separating the hand from the face. This movement upward increases the feeling of weight of the body and emphasizes the pull toward the feet.

little crucifixion by Norbert Smith. Top award in Michiana Art Exhibition, South Bend Art Center, South Bend, Indiana.

statement by critic

Intellectual symbolism was the concept which probably demanded the judge's favor toward this representation of the Crucifixion. But the distinctive beauty of this artist's work would probably win judge, jury or critic anywhere.

judge

William D. Peat, John Herron Art Museum.

jane stauffer

Miss Stauffer is now a fashion illustrator and a teacher of children's classes at the Montgomery Museum of Fine Arts, Montgomery, Alabama.

statement by the artist

Wind and Rock is an illustration for "Fragment" by Gerard Manley Hopkins. Hopkins' "Fragment" is a four-line poem composed of forceful imagery which conveys the elemental strength of the wind. The poem is constructed of abstract word combinations, such as "strike, churl" and "giant air." In order to produce an effective visual representation, I used abstractions from the forms of nature. My approach had to reflect the vitality and strength of the poetry.

The two unsuccessful oil paintings which were attempts to illustrate "Fragment" proved invaluable as references in executing the final illustration. The first painting was not a satisfactory solution because the composition, colors and shapes were contrived; the second was not a fresh, vital statement. A combination of media . . . paint and collage involving the use of enamel, varnish, paper and burlap . . . is employed to communicate my individual experience.

Beginning directly on the canvas, I slashed free lines of black enamel with the handle of a brush; these lines served as a framework for the composition. The fluid tonal areas in transparent browns were achieved by the use of several varnish stains; torn, textured papers and frayed pieces of burlap were then introduced; white enamel was scumbled over certain areas of the paper and burlap. After continuing and alternating the three techniques until a rich tonal effect was produced, I felt the collage was a mature statement, although large areas of the canvas were exposed. The bare canvas in certain areas contributes to the fresh quality in the over-all visual effect.

Design-wise, the strong verticals suggest trees and the horizontals, the earth. The light areas moving horizontally allude to the action of the wind. The visual advancing and receding of the planes, created by the value contrasts, bring a more fluid feeling to the representation.

critic's comments

Wind and rock, force and resistance, tangible and intangible, feeling and form, movement and solidity: the contrast of these pairs of elements has had a long history in the traditional problems of painting. Like the wind, man's thought, feeling and perception, remain unknown unless some action is taken, some material affected, some movement is made.

Like the white sheet of paper laid over the lodestone that creates a magnetic field, the painter thinks of his canvas as a field of force. As the iron filings dropped on the paper are directed by the magnet and make the limits of the field apparent, so do the materials of the painter assume patterns that are indications both of psychical and physical tensions on the canvas. We do not see the field, only the evidence of its reality; we do not see the tensions, we feel them; there is no movement, but we interpret the tendencies as such.

In the painting, *Wind and Rock*, material such as burlap has been used to indicate solidity and resistance to the stated and implied axial lines of the planes, the burlap offering by its textured right angles of warp and woof a terminus for the movement, further accentuating the resistance to the force. This painting directs our attention beyond the realm of appearances and into one of the mysteries of existence.

wind and rock by Jane Stauffer. Top award in 51st Annual Birmingham Art Association Jury Exhibition, Birmingham Museum of Art, Birmingham, Alabama.

statement by critic

One has only to observe the technical detail of this painting to see why the judge probably picked it. Analyze, too, how everything in the painting harmonizes and interconnects . . . allowing the color to outline the forms, thus avoiding stiffness.

judge

Josef Albers, Yale University.

william radford thomas

Mr. Thomas is currently Chairman of the
San Antonio Men of Art Guild,
San Antonio, Texas.

statement by the artist

As I stop to consider my "philosophy" I am confronted with paintings that do not tie me personally with my area but which seem to fit in with any given area with which I am familiar.

This non-regional characteristic seems to derive itself from a way of thinking rather than any material person, place or thing. Of course, thinking is partly made up of past experiences, which gives them an indirect value in controlling our thought mechanisms. However, as one gains new experiences, old ones are quite often integrated or entirely eliminated from the consciousness. The "new" thought process can then isolate the individual from his original environment.

As for painting, one may even lose the conscious knowledge of past experiences when applying or mixing paint. I believe this is an ideal state, since the artist is then free to apply his thought to more intrinsic problems related to his aims or goals.

In my specific opinion, one of the more important goals is that of reflecting the general time or world attitude. The faces with which I feel so attached contain more to me than just mere figure representation; they even contain more than solid composition, which of itself is extremely important. These faces are a culmination of my experiences and thoughts as conceived at the moment of creation.

Further, a painting must transmit a magical quality so that even when far removed from the artist or his time, the magical something is quite evident to the audience. Make no mistake. The audience is not important or even considered during the creative process. But on the other hand, where would society be if the creative process did not exist?

All this means that as a painter I am concerned with the labor of my own making.

critic's comments

It is not unusual to hear or read of analogies between the child and the artist. Frequently, lay critical opinion, in comparing the two, is not too kind to the work of the adult, much favoring the products of his own five-year-old, to what to him is the meaningless dribble and splotches of a chronologically mature adult.

Just as the child's play seems to be directed toward no practical end, so does a great deal of painting appear to the business world to be nothing but child's play. The vocation of painting is still suspect as a profession for a "grown man."

This is, perhaps, more true of painting than of any of the other arts. The inherent danger here is in the blind acceptance of the unquestioned presupposition that would equate adjustment to conformity. For painting is a means of adjustment for both child and artist, a means of correlating physical skills with knowledge and perception. What differentiates the child from the man is the man's level of reducing the contingencies of his work to convey and impose on others his own particular vision.

PHOTO BY MARTHA MOOD

a whole childhood of fantasy lies ahead by William Radford Thomas. Top award in Texas Annual Painting & Sculpture Exhibition, Dallas Museum of Fine Arts, Dallas, Texas.

This is a beguilingly deceptive painting. The immediate image of the child offers no difficulty, nor what the child has been doing, but what strikes us with its profundity is that the image of the child is emerging from what he has been doing. Because of his conquest of the outside world in terms of his "marks," he is adding to his being.

Because of the kind of space in this painting we cannot be satisfied by simply feeling that the child is standing in front of a wall. Rather, the space argues that the child has been painting on a glass or mirror. If a mirror, he is confronting himself within a world of his own making. If a glass, he is confronting us with a world which we have lost the capacity to understand.

statement by the judge

The Thomas painting I considered distinguished for its strange and somewhat ominous sense of color, a unique combination of brushstroke and design, developed with the figure into a form of psychological portrait. It is strong, well executed, and challenging.

LAURENCE SCHMECKEBIER
Professor of Fine Arts, and Director, School of Art,
Syracuse University, Syracuse, New York

105

robert
vickers

Mr. Vickers is now Associate Professor of Fine Arts at Ohio Wesleyan University, where he teaches drawing, design (studio), and primitive art (lecture) and is a director of exhibitions. He is listed in Who's Who in American Art.

statement by the artist

I think I believe in what I understand, and I can only work and wonder at that which I do not understand. Painting is a region of mythic wonderment, and it seems that only painting tells me what I really want to know. I do not care why a painting happens. It is more important that it does happen, and this starts with work. To work is the important thing. The term, creative process, is repelling, and I am more concerned with the destructive process.

The bare canvas is a big space. I move in nothingness for as long as I can. I turn around, and if a long time later I can see it between my eyes, I am glad, and it is done.

The painting, *Chateau in Winter*, grew from the work rather than the work from the idea. It did not evolve from remembrances of any particular structure, but instead out of the sense of a powerful and sprawling monstrousness inside a great quiet. I have seen Pierrefonds, Amboise and many other chateaux, but their effect is all the same . . . monsters which were not built but were slowly pushed up from the center of the earth by non-human hands . . . when no one was looking . . . until their presence became dominant over a land. I had worked with something of this in mind on perhaps a half dozen canvases. I felt a solid, almost stolid virtue to be in a great and quiet strength which dominates but does not dictate . . . like a medieval fortress in the dead of winter.

In looking backward, perhaps the real founding sense is one of animism.

critic's comments

One need not know the title of this painting in order to feel the sharp cold or to remember the somber purple twilights of winter, where the whites of snow tentatively blot up and reflect the sober tones around it, remnants of tone from an autumn already cast aside.

This employment of planes to evoke variations in mood can also be found in the work of the late Niles Spencer as well as some of the more severe works of Charles Sheeler. Though the work here marks a distinct turn from its origin in the school of "Suprematism" by its atmospheric qualities, it still maintains an emphasis on the formal means of picture making.

Today, we hear much of the return of "subject matter," that painters are going back to "content" in their pictures, as though there were definite progressive directions, as if all development were unilateral. This "return," this "going back" smacks of the Victorian idea of human progress as the result of historic necessity, and is misleading when applied to the arts, to say the least. Industrial procedures, scientific theories, and empiric philosophies can become obsolete because there are facts and efficiencies involved. But in painting, once a feeling becomes a fact, the survival of the picture as art may well depend on the will-temperament traits of the painter.

Chateau in Winter has abjured the diagonals used by Spencer to create a sense of deeper space, not because this artist is returning to or from Mondrian, but because he found those diagonals incompatible with the feeling he wished to create with the forms at his disposal.

chateau in winter by Robert Vickers. Top award, Artists of Southern Ohio, Dayton, Ohio.

statements by judges

Chateau in Winter is marked by a strong sense of design. The colors and shapes are well integrated and balanced to produce a genuine work of art expressed in contemporary terms.

GORDON M. SMITH, Director
Albright Art Gallery

A clear vision painted with certainty. Clean, it seems to be exactly what the painter wanted it to be.

HEDDA STERN, Painter

judges

Hedda Stern, New York City; Gordon MacIntosh Smith, Albright Art Gallery, Buffalo, New York.

107

gordon wagner

Mr. Wagner now lives in
Topanga, California.

statement by the artist

Living in and around nature . . . seeing organics and feeling the changing elements . . . these things consistently lead me into extracting from nature for the basic elements of my paintings.

I have studied and associated with several groups of the so-called "primitive people of America" and have found their cultures to be in complete harmony with nature. It may be called witchcraft, soothsaying, or magic. I prefer to call art magic, regardless of the medium. Nature's accidents are tossed upon the beach daily by the sea. Rocks, bent iron, broken glass, a water-worn stick with a random paint splotch dripped on it, are some of the examples.

A piece of wood will be overlooked by many passers-by. Then one person will stop, scrutinize it only for an instant. Many more people will pass by until the man who passed the first time returns and feels a possessive glow toward it.

The painting, Sky Festival, is a compilation of many observations. It was executed with spontaneity and intuitiveness . . . and was as personal as the man culling the pieces of wood on the beach. It depicts the Indian way, and combines all the basic elements of air, water, fire, and magic. The serpentine-like forms express motion of the dancers in universal harmony. Painting Sky Festival was a wonderful moment of nostalgia.

critic's comments

With contemporary civilization's ever-expanding eclecticism operating within the agencies of anthropology and archaeology, the museum, that reflecting mind of society, presents for our contemplation the control as well as the functional lassitude of object and image in the milieu from which it originates. Such a presentation may cause in the mind of today's painter either a yearning for the past or the present primitive wherein his function would be more integrated (and less discrete). But here is a paradox. The very freedom which sponsors the objective eclecticism of science is the same freedom which permits the painter's nostalgia for a more meaningful position in society. Instead of being born into a function to find his freedom within the strict limitations imposed, he must redefine his function and fulfill his purpose and find his being within his own definition.

The eye that even unconsciously approaches Sky Festival from the Greco-Renaissance aesthetic will come away baffled, because there is no image to use as a means of entering the painting. Once the categorical "ought" of what we should be able to see or to find in the painting is disposed of, the participation of the spectator is greatly facilitated.

This composition is based on a design roughly "H" in shape, and it is this shape which becomes an object of awareness as it separates from the less-solid forms surrounding it. Because of the heaviness of the red, there is a tendency for this color to move down toward the base of the painting in opposition to the lighter shapes that are pushing, like air bubbles, to the top. These two movements give added impetus and vitality to the black and yellow forms that dance in opposition to the major tensions. These patterns become more and more meaningful, once the discipline imposed on them becomes more apparent.

sky festival by Gordon Wagner. Top award in Exhibition of the Annual for Artists in the Western States, Denver, Colorado.

statement by critic

The judge probably decided in favor of this painting because of the dazzling and vivid color . . . the smooth rhythm.

judge

Lee Malone, Houston Museum of Fine Arts, Houston, Texas.

john wheat

Mr. Wheat is now living in Stamford, Connecticut. He is listed in Who's Who in American Art.

statement by the artist

I start painting by forming a structure in which imagery grows into being. I paint what comes to me emotionally. I try to express the universal aspect of things, to explore the subconscious, to plumb the depths of creativeness, to understand compulsions and inject some of the knowledge or emotions thus uncovered into paintings to provide a personal, spiritual and individual message. There are a million years behind us to be expressed, and an eon ahead undiscovered.

I am a romanticist. A romantic painter. Art to me is neither peaceful nor pure.

Nature to me provides a spring-board for knowledge, pleasure and pain in fathoming problems related to the great creative forces, truths out of which man discovers a natural validity.

I painted *The Conqueror* first as an emotional structure encompassing the world of man. Man and The Universe. Man against a universe which is neither rational nor just. Man who has courage in the face of certain disaster, whose courage makes for spiritual victory.

critic's comments

It is as though the soul, in turning from the noon's light, seals itself from the eye's color, the bent brilliance of reflecting materiality, to journey inward into those deep darks of exceeding richness, and there in solitude and loneliness, in a battle without action, save the slip of time on time, moment on moment, confronts the bulwarks of the unknown with the assertion that its own forces contain the question and the answer of its origin and destiny. Thus it was when the aging Titian flayed the rustic Marsyas and hung his pitiful mortality to a tree in answer to the touching music that was far too god-like; thus it was in the soundless world that Goya brought forth those monsters bred by the sleep of reason, whose black wings still brush the scruff of stiff-necked man; thus it was in the everlasting twilight pressing against the eternal night, Rembrandt saw the solitary rider on a pale horse. And his name was Titus and also Death.

The Conqueror sits with grave dignity on his charger, contemplating the image of his helmet which he has removed. In his left hand he carries a lance. The lowered head of the horse becomes ominously predatory because of the deep shadows cast by its protecting armor. The entire composition is made up of interlocking ellipses balanced against angular contrasts of light and dark. By the paint application one might be persuaded that this is an "expressionist" painting, but further examination proves this not to be the truth, for the drawing is classical, the space resolved, and the color restrained. Further, the iconography being the traditional "Death on a Pale Horse," takes the symbolism out of the problematical realm of the subjective and places it in the more severe line of objective development.

"And I looked, and behold a pale horse: and his name that sat on him as Death, and Hell followed with him. And power was given unto them over the fourth part of the earth, to kill with sword, and with hunger, and with death, and with the beasts of the earth." Revelation 6:8.

the conqueror by John Wheat. Top award in Exhibition of the Connecticut Academy of Fine Arts, Morgan Memorial, Hartford, Connecticut.

John Wheat paints realistically. That is, the theme and the details of his compositions are crystal clear to any observer, so clear in fact that the parts seem almost an illusion. In painting a scene, say a moody winter day, does he sit at his window, look across snow-laden fields and then reproduce what appears before him? He does not. In such a case, his code dictates that he paint "the essence of winter—the spirit of all winters everywhere—the impression of winter registered on the minds of all the generations of our ancestors back to the start of the human race." Naturally he doesn't expect to realize fully such a directive, but he holds it as a goal to which all artists might reasonably aspire. He feels Brueghel came nearer to such registration of composite winter than any other painter.

His serious compositions are always developed in the studio. The outdoors is used only for inspiration and factual detail reference.

As with winter scenes, so also with other themes! Instead of attempting to record fleeting, factual impressions of nature's moods, he thinks artists should "strive to depict the *universal appearance* of things, to explore the subconscious mind, to plumb the depths of our creativeness, to understand our inner compulsions and inject some of the knowledge or emotions thus uncovered into paintings to provide a personal, spiritual and individual message for there are a million years of humanity behind us to be expressed."

FREDERIC WHITAKER, "John Wheat," in the *American Artist*, September, 1957.

judges

Revington Arthur, Glenbrook, Connecticut; Kenneth Bates, Mystic, Connecticut; Gladys Bates, Mystic, Connecticut; Isabel Bishop, Riverdale, New York; Norman Kent, New York City.

PHOTO BY LEN PROVATO